On Call for God
Experiences of a Hospital Chaplain

Mirelle van der Zyl

On Call for God
Experiences of a Hospital Chaplain

By

Mirella van der Zyl

Photographs © Ernest van der Zyl

Printed by Lulu Press, Inc.

All Bible passages are from the NIV (New International Version) Bible.

To Ernest, my faithful husband and helpmate

Contents

Introduction

In the course of their careers, chaplains are often required to be on duty after traditional working hours, a circumstance commonly known as being "on call." Equipped with mobile technologies like pagers and cell phones, they make themselves available, ready to go to the scene of an emergency, whatever it may be. They assess the situation and offer appropriate assistance as required. Their experience and training guide them, and their faith inspires them.

Having spent most of my career working in hospitals, I can remember walking through quiet corridors and observing how the light cast an eerie shadow on everything. I lifted my heart to God and asked him to be present during the task that awaited me. In those tense moments during emergency calls, I knew I stood there representing God. Perhaps I brought his promise of everlasting peace to someone whose life was ending, providing assurance of hope in God to someone in great anguish upon receiving a fatal diagnosis, or offering God's comfort to the patient's family.

As I relate some of my experiences in my chaplaincy, it now occurs to me that I wasn't just offering spiritual care to the many people whose paths I crossed. I was offering myself to help God in his work, so that I was, in essence, on call for God.

As you read, you will find that I use God in the masculine gender. I have been brought up that way, and it has always been a comfort to me to address God as my Father, but I've also referred to God as the Supreme Being, the Sustainer, and Creator of All Things. I'm very aware that, to some people, the reference to God as being distinctly male is inconsistent with their beliefs. Therefore, I have come to respect other representations of God, for instance, as female or Supreme Power of the Universe. After all, as the sentiment has been expressed many times before, it may be that we all believe in the same God, but we use different practices in our worship

During my recent vacation, early in the morning, the lake—a seemingly endless expanse of pristine water that glittered with streaks of gold from the rising sun—was still. Nothing stirred. It was a place of absolute calm and tranquility, and my soul rejoiced. I had just retired from my career, and a day with no obligations and nothing to do lie ahead of me. I contentedly sat by the lake and let my thoughts wander.

It was the perfect time to communicate with the Lord and take stock of my life under his guidance. I had achieved a lot in my life. My career in ministry started when I was sixteen years old and brought me to serve as a chaplain for over twenty years. Many dreams had been fulfilled; many prayers were answered. I was satisfied with my life and could name few regrets. But what lay ahead? I worried a little about how I would occupy my time now that so many obligations and responsibilities lay behind me. After getting up in the morning and going to work for so many years, striving tirelessly to realize my dreams and goals, how would I fill my days?

Something inside me stirred, and out of it came a message that said, "Look inside your dreams." When I did, I realized that not all of them had been fulfilled. When I was a teenager, I said I would be a writer one day. The dream called out to me again.

My elementary school teacher had often read my stories aloud to my class and used them as an example of how my classmates should write. At the time, I didn't realize the impact of what she was doing, but now that I thought about it, I wondered, "Was I that good then?"

Admittedly, the task was rather difficult. I wasn't writing in my mother tongue, Italian, but in my second language. Despite the challenge to write in English, some force within me compelled me to write what was in my heart. A dear friend confirmed it by saying, "If it makes you happy, why not pursue it?" Thus it brought me joy to document some of my past experiences, reflections, achievements, mistakes, and things I learned.

The first three chapters of the book relate my experiences with patients of all ages, from children to the elderly. Chapter four explores the difficult challenges that death presents to all of us. The fifth chapter examines the role the chapel plays in a health-care facility. Finally, in the last chapter, I offer a tribute to the many people who had an influence on both my life and career.

I hope that some young clergy, pastoral visitors, or fledgling chaplains might read my writing and be led to a solution to their questions and challenges, some example they could apply to their work, or some kind of support.

When I was sixteen, I decided to follow Christ with all my gifts in order to get the best preparation. I served in my father's church in southern Italy, and I've never looked back. I've had times of doubt, questioning, and frustration, but I could honestly say I have followed Christ all my life in several ministries. I remain open to the opportunities for service he has placed before me.

In my younger years, I lacked confidence and knowledge. One of my teachers told me several times, "Mirella, when you do not know what to do, follow your gut. Your instincts will guide you." He was so right. Even now, in this endeavor, when I doubted my capacity to accomplish something, his words echoed within me, "Follow your gut."

Having gone through the process of chaplaincy, I faced many situations and experienced confusion in parts of my ministry. At times, I didn't know what to do and felt at a loss for words of comfort and assurance. Perhaps some of those instances and the way I handled them may provide insight to my readers about what they might do or choose to do differently.

I truly loved the years I spent as a chaplain, even more than those spent in pastoral service at my church. The challenges those experiences presented forced me to call upon everything I had learned, to continually develop and sharpen my skills, but also to display compassion and patience and offer the comfort and support that was asked.

If my words can encourage readers and give them a sense of direction as they start their own ministry, provide comfort or inspiration to someone facing medical treatments, or simply offer insight and perspective in pastoral care, then my dream will be fulfilled, and my soul will sing the joyful song that comes from having helped someone else.

At times, I left a patient's bedside with the feeling I hadn't really done anything useful or helpful. Yet, I had to submit to the Lord what I had done and let him use it for his purpose. Perhaps you have experienced this as well. If so, I hope you don't feel discouraged for too long. Place your efforts in the Lord's hands, whatever they are, and he will put them to good use.

Acknowledgments

It took a long time to compose this book, and I've had the help and support of friends and family to journey with me. Because I'm deeply thankful to them, I'll mention them here. Heather Price faithfully placed the manuscript on the computer even after I had lost a draft. My precious son Will van der Zyl, despite a heavy schedule of his own, painstakingly edited my first draft. Carolyn Wilker of FineTune Editing, Kitchener, edited my manuscript for submission. Gary Chalk, the director of public affairs at Brant Community Health Care Centre, read my manuscript and presented some of my stories to the *Expositor*, the local newspaper. Sister Kathleen O'Neill of the congregation of St. Joseph in Hamilton, teaching supervisor for Cappe, read my manuscript and gave me her opinion. Mrs. Elisabeth Morrison read it, too, and contributed her ideas. My darling daughter Giselle Loder gave continuous help with my computer problems in reviewing my manuscript. I thank my faithful husband for his innumerable times of help and support in many ways. The Word Alive Press short-listed my manuscript in the Winnipeg contest of the year. I thank the Word Guild for the consultation with their editors and publishers about my book. Dr. Ross Pennie of the Brant Community Health Care Centre gave some sound advice, and I thank many others who contributed in small ways to encourage me to publish my book.

Chapter 1

And Jesus Blessed the Children

One of the greatest challenges health-care professionals face while providing care is in not allowing themselves to be emotionally overwhelmed by the suffering and discomfort that their patients experience. This is especially difficult when the people facing serious illness are children. We would all agree that it is particularly heartbreaking when people so young, who are only starting what should be a long and healthy life, are diagnosed with a terminal illness or suffer serious injury.

My first experience working with children took place in the neurological ward at the Hospital for Sick Children in Toronto in 1985. I felt quite apprehensive, not knowing how I could help or how capable I might be. However, I was also very curious and eager to learn. For instance, I learned that children with hydrocephalus needed shunts implanted in their skulls when they were born, only to have them replaced with larger ones as they grew. For those children, this meant many trips to the hospital throughout their childhood.

I also learned that children could go into comas, often for many weeks, due to accidents with their bikes or from other playtime activities. Some children emerged from the trauma quite well and were able to continue normal lives, while others had to relearn everything. It was always a miracle to see a child wake up from a coma. I thought of it as a resurrection. Children who had problems with their nervous systems experienced slowed growth that also prevented them from enjoying normal lives. All these aspects of sickness and more were truly shocking to me. I had never thought that they could happen to children.

My greatest sense of compassion went to the parents. What a journey they went through with their children! What pain they endured because they loved their children so much and had to leave them in the hospital. I witnessed many agonizing good-byes at night when parents had to leave their child crying in a crib and calling with outstretched arms. So many tears and sobs happened in those little beds. I would often gently caress their little heads and softly sing to get them to sleep.

How blessed I felt that my children were all healthy, growing well, and safely at home with their father. How insignificant their misbehavior seemed compared to the pain and sickness I saw around me, pain that seemed unfairly inflicted upon these children and their families.

At night, in the silence of the ward, I prayed in my heart that Jesus would take them all on his knee and bless them with a good night of sleep and they would already feel a little better when they awoke the next morning.

Playing on the Tracks

All too often, terrible things happen to children that cause their parents to wonder, "If only …" Forever after, they are saddled with bitterness and sorrow at such occurrences or the regret that they might have somehow been able to prevent the accident. Whenever I became involved in such tragedies, I would pray that God would give me the courage to effectively handle the devastating situation.

This was the case in the emergency room (ER) at Brantford General Hospital (BGH) when I was called in late one morning. I found it ironic that, on such a day, when the sun was shining and the day promised to be a good one, there could be such a tragedy. A group of people had assembled in the corridor outside the emergency room, and they were arguing loudly amongst themselves. One of the nurses briefed me that Jason, a fourteen-year-old boy, had been brought in and declared dead. Jason and a friend had been following the railway tracks outside of town. Jason had jumped on a slow-moving train. Elated, he had yelled to his friend below to join him. He had not seen another train coming on the track next to him. The oncoming train hit him and killed him instantly, while his friend was able to stay off the tracks.

The family was gathered around him. It took me a while to sort out their relationship to him. It was a big family with one parent, a stepfather, and a number of uncles, aunts, and grandmothers. They were yelling at each other, shouting how this accident should not have happened. I stepped among them, trying to be heard. They eventually realized I was there to help. The nurses had asked me to please keep them a little quieter, as they were disturbing the other patients.

I requested that the boy's biological parent, grandmother, and one of his siblings stay with him. I talked gently to them about the peace that God gives to those he loves. They were numb with grief and shock, and I wasn't sure they could accept what I was saying. I prayed with them for comfort in this time of great agony and confusion, when they asked so many questions but no answers were provided.

I left them by the bedside and joined the rest of the family in the hall. There, too, I tried to bring some order to their grief. One of the grandmothers was so angry and in shock that did not know what she was saying while she shouted, "Why wasn't he in school? What was he doing out there? Playing on the trains? Didn't he know how dangerous it was? Where have they put him? I'm gonna kill him for all this."

She cried in my arms, and then another relative spoke angrily, "Where's his friend? He's so safe now. Look at our boy. Why this? It isn't right."

His words made me shudder. "Is it not a good thing that at least one life was spared? I know it isn't right for you to have lost your boy, but imagine having two deaths on our hands."

Of course, my words brought little comfort and did not calm the anger and hatred that poured out of these family members. It took more than two hours to sort out things with the police, the Children's Aid Society, and the other agencies called in for this tragic accident.

I went back to the parents, who, by this time, were arguing over whose fault it was that Jason did not go to school every day as he was supposed to and why he was running around all day, playing dangerous games.

I quietly went to a corner and asked God for guidance and the ability to bring comfort when my heart was torn between anger and the inability to comprehend all that was happening. As I went back to the family, I noticed some were leaving. Others were talking in hushed tones among themselves. The parents were quiet now. They sat in the boy's room and listened as the doctor talked to them. I thanked God for his intervention, for reestablishing some normalcy in the midst of tragedy.

At the end of the day, I was exhausted. It had taken long talks with the family, each member in turn, to help them find some sense of peace. They had left, one by one, to go home and deal with the situation in the best way they knew. Knowing they received support from different agencies, I placed them all in the Lord's hands to guide them in the days ahead.

How can we deal with the death of one so young? How do we reconcile the thought that carelessness and reckless behavior brought about the death? Despite our best efforts to teach our children of the dangers in life, how do we get them to use their better judgment and avoid risky situations? I can only pray and believe that God, in his mercy, had gathered Jason to his breast and sent angels to comfort the stricken family.

Matthew

In the silence of the nights at the hospital, when the lights are dim and the children are asleep in their beds, it's very conducive for talking quietly with parents and families. Mothers and fathers share their long, painful journeys of their children's sickness. They can't leave their children alone at night, but stay to watch over their children as they sleep, offering their prayers and their love.

Matthew, an eleven-year-old boy from Southern Europe, had an illness that the doctors could not clearly diagnose. He couldn't walk and speak, and he was blind. Because Matthew's mother didn't speak English, and therefore couldn't communicate with hospital staff, the boy's aunt came to the hospital and stayed with him most of the time. I spoke to her in Spanish, and she told me how much they had struggled with Matthew to help him get better. I had visited the boy several times and always found him thrashing and groaning in his bed.

After that, I talked softly to him in Spanish. The family said he'd understand. I sang a lullaby I knew and caressed his forehead. In minutes, he calmed down and seemed to listen. Oh, the expression of wonder and intense pleasure that came over his face!

His aunt told me that he loved to listen to the music on the radio while moving about on the floor. He had no device to help him stand or move by himself, and his aunt was trying to find out what was available that would help him. I admired her faith in the nurses and doctors and her determination to seek help for her nephew, even though she wasn't his primary caregiver. She described the continuous stress on Matthew's family to deal with his tantrums and his lack of cooperation. She said how stressed his mother was, looking after her family, holding a job, and caring for Matthew in the evening.

I prayed several times with his aunt and other members of the family that Jesus would hold this severely handicapped child in his arms and give the family the wisdom they needed to look after him in the appropriate way. While I do not know what happened to Matthew, I hope that, when he returned home, he was able to receive the help he needed to enjoy a better life.

Miracles

I witnessed miracles in the children's ward that filled my heart with joy and faith. Often, children who had lapsed into a coma were brought in.

A truck had hit seven-year-old Tim while he rode his bicycle. At the time, it wasn't mandatory for children to wear helmets while riding their bikes. Tim had suffered a severe head injury, so the doctors only gave him a 20 percent chance of survival.

While in a coma, Tim neither awoke nor did anything for several weeks. He gradually started to blink his eyes, and he opened them one day. He only focused on his parents. It was a miracle, and they cried with joy and hugged him.

One day, not long after this breakthrough, I was talking to him and noticed he focused on me for a while, listening to my words. The nurses told me how quickly he was improving. No longer was he someone with only a 20 percent chance of survival. Now that he'd begun to respond, he moved, drank, and ate, even if the food was light. When I visited one day, I thought he looked at me and smiled. I couldn't believe my eyes. I turned around to tell the nurse. Behind me was Tim's dad. Tim had smiled at him. We rejoiced together at this miraculous return to life. In fact, it wasn't long before Tim was packing his things to go back home. He still had ways to go to reach his pre-accident state, but the recovery he had made was miraculous. I was then reminded of Jesus' commandment to feed his sheep who are suffering and to journey with them in their pain and anguish.

Laura

The mood was relaxed and pleasant as a group of us enjoyed our coffee at the shop of Tim Horton's in BGH. We chatted happily with each other until we heard an announcement on the public address system, asking for a pediatrician to go to the ER "stat," meaning a child was in danger. We pensively resumed our conversation. Then after a few more minutes, we heard another call … for pastoral care in ER. That call was for me. Everyone in the group fell silent. They knew what it meant. A child was dying or dead. Such a call involves a lot of people. When a person is in ER, the situation is quite serious, but, when it's a child, it's especially difficult to bear.

I hurried to the ER and found the parents of a little girl, Laura, in tremendous distress. They had just brought her in from home, and she had already been pronounced dead on arrival (DOA). A minor illness in the previous few days didn't seem serious enough for the parents to miss work, so they had left Laura with her grandparents. Laura had grown sicker, and her worried grandparents had taken her to the hospital. They called Laura's parents at work and told them to come quickly to the ER at BGH. That's where the parents found their little girl lying lifeless, as in a deep sleep.

The atmosphere was frenetic with their cries of anguish, the glare of bright lights, and the bustle of the staff coming and going. I tried to bring some calm. Then I called their priest, Father Don.

He came quickly and recognized the parents. He had performed their marriage ceremony and baptized Laura. With great compassion, he talked to them as if they were his children. He blessed them, anointed Laura, and bent to kiss her with infinite tenderness.

I couldn't hold in my tears. So when Laura's mother looked at me, she came and put her arms around me. We cried together, and Father Don spoke tenderly to both of us. Though it was a terrible tragedy, Father Don had brought great tenderness and calm to everyone in that room.

Later in my office, I thought of Laura, the little golden-haired girl who had died. An autopsy had been ordered because the cause of her death was uncertain. Following that procedure, Father Don would look after Laura's funeral and her family.

Laura looked very much like my granddaughter Grace, who was about the same age. I thought of my precious little Grace when she would come to me and want to sit on my lap. The thought of losing her was unbearable, and I shed more tears for Laura.

At that moment, there was great pain in my heart, but also anger toward the traumas to which my work exposed me. I had to face situations so painful that it was almost impossible to detach myself. I had to, or the alternative was to quit my job. Thinking long and hard, I knew that quitting wasn't the solution and wouldn't bring me peace. The only answer was to continue in my work where confronting pain and anguish would make me more attuned with the suffering of patients and their families.

Tiny Bundles and Empty Arms

My grandchildren sometimes come to me all at once. I gather them in my arms. We laugh, giggle, and squeal. They are such a precious bunch that they fill my arms and my heart with joy. I kiss them tenderly. Then I let them go again to their play. I feel so blessed with my children and my grandchildren for all the richness of love and care that comes from all of them.

I remember the day my children were born, how tenderly I held them for the first time, how perfectly they fit in my arms, and how they filled my heart with joy and love. I remember the expression of great tenderness and awe in my husband's face when he held his son, ready to take him home from the hospital. Our arms have always been full with children to love and raise.

How does a mother feel when that bliss is taken away from her? For several months, she carries a new life in her womb, feels it grow, kick, quiver, and move. Then an unexpected complication occurs, and the baby is born prematurely.

With the advances in the science and medicine of today come the increased chances that the little life can survive, even though there may be problems. But other times, the fetus does not survive. The baby is born lifeless with a horrible purple color. The baby is a little, completely formed body with very small limbs.

Many times late at night or early in the morning, a doctor called me to spend time with the family. The scene was always heart-wrenching. A mother held and kissed her baby and cried over the tiny, inert body. The other members of the family were unable to hold back their tears. Their pain was unbearable. There was no hope, just the cruel reality of a little body with no life.

It always disturbed me deeply. Many times, I couldn't hold my own tears and cried with them. Then I gathered all my strength and courage to ask about the parents' and family's wishes. They sometimes wanted the baby baptized; they sometimes wanted just a blessing placed upon him or her.

Each time, I'd draw on my faith and talk of how Jesus blessed the children a long time ago and still does so now. He gathered the little one, just born, into his arms and took the child, happy and completely alive, into the kingdom of heaven. I told them how God extended his blessing to the family, day by day, to help them deal with their loss. And I would baptize the little one in the mother's arms while the rest of the family looked on. The child looked so cute wearing the little bonnet and outfit the nurse had put on him or her. I would name the child as the parents wished, and I would bless the baby, too. Then I'd bless the whole family, especially the parents, that they might hold onto hope for better days in the future

I always placed great meaning on the little one who had come, how important he or she was in his family's life, and how deeply he or she put a seal on his or her parents' hearts. It was usually a brief, painful ceremony with everyone present, both staff and family, expressing powerful emotions.

Of all the expressions of pain that I have witnessed, the pain of parents who lose a child is the most profound because there is no hope for that child. An adult has already lived his or her life to a certain extent, but a child is at the very beginning or has not even started. I think of how that new mother must feel. I believe Jesus blesses the children who go to him too early and he gives them a full life in his kingdom. I also believe that Jesus takes the tears of those parents who grieve their loss and transforms them into a feeling of hope for a new life in the future. In those years of assistance to bereaved parents, I grew in my appreciation and love for children at every age and from every walk of life.

I help to raise my grandchildren with all the patience, wisdom, and love I can find in myself. When they come to me, calling me, "Nonna, Nonna," my heart leaps with joy at the sight of them, for they represent a continuation of my life, as do all of God's children.

There Is Hope in the Air

On one of those bitterly cold nights, I had retired early to my room in one of the Hospitals in Toronto. I fell asleep quickly because I'd had a busy day with many visits. Then my pager went off and suddenly woke me up. I prepared myself for a call to the emergency room. As always, I said a fervent prayer to the Lord to make me an instrument of his love.

As I reached the ER, I heard loud wailing and screaming. I entered the quiet room reserved for family and met two ladies in great distress. One was wailing loudly; the other was trying to comfort her. I went to the ER to get the report. One of the nurses told me they had brought in Jeremy, a fourteen-year-old boy who had suffered a head injury. He had been snowboarding with his friends. While coming down a treacherous slope, he had been unable to stop and eventually hit his head on a parked bus. The fact he hadn't worn a helmet made this moment more difficult.

Jeremy lay unconscious and naked on an examining table under the stark white lights while a team of doctors and nurses worked on him. They did not know yet what his chances of survival would be. The nurse advised me to stay with his mother and asked if I could calm her down.

I went back to the quiet room. By this time, the two women were a bit calmer, but the boy's mother was still sobbing. I introduced myself, asked their names, and then sat beside Marta, Jeremy's mother. The second lady, her sister, assured Marta that she would take care of Emma, Jeremy's sister, who was still at home with a neighbor. After a while, she left to pick up Emma.

Marta told me that she and her husband had been separated, but she should go and call him about their son.

"Oh, so much trouble since he left us. Jeremy just runs in the street with a bunch of boys, and I've had a hard time to control him. I have to work, so I'm not home with Emma and Jeremy all the time. I have to raise them all alone because he decided to leave us. There was someone else more interesting than us," she told me between sobs.

"I'm sorry, Marta. Now we have to think of Jeremy. Let's just wait for the doctors to finish their work and pray. Let's pray as faithfully as we can."

Marta went to phone her husband. I got some water and tissues for her. We both returned to the stark, gray confines of that room to await the doctor's report. After a while, we heard a pounding on the door and an angry voice. I went to see what was happening and found a large man talking to a nurse in the hall, demanding to see his son. I gathered he was Jeremy's father, and I ushered him into the quiet room.

"There you are. You let my son go out in the street. Look what happens!"

"Calm down, Culbert. He was just out playing for a while. I can't keep him in the house all the time."

"Where's Emma?"

"She's with my sister. She's safe. Let's calm down and wait and pray. The chaplain is with us. She has been with me all this time."

He sat in a corner, grumbling and weeping. I left them to inquire in the ER. The nurse said that Jeremy had opened his eyes and his vitals were getting steadier. It was encouraging news.

"There are good signs." I reentered the quiet room.

Both parents looked at me expectantly and wiped tears from their eyes.

"Jeremy has opened his eyes, and his vital signs are better."

"Thank the Lord." Marta covered her face with her hands.

I put my arms around her and explained that Jeremy still needed help.

"Well, Marta, he's going to make it. He's our son, a good boy. I always said that." Culbert jumped up and approached Marta. "Now, don't upset yourself so much. You know it isn't good for you."

After another hour, the doctor came in and announced that Jeremy was conscious. As far as he could tell, he had a severe concussion, but the X-ray didn't show any broken bones.

Culbert took the doctor's hand and shook it firmly. "Praise the Lord. Thank you, doctor. It's so good to hear you say that."

"Can we see him?" Marta asked.

"Yes, but just for a few minutes. We'll keep him in observation for a while. Come now."

We followed the doctor to the ER, and Marta reached Jeremy's bedside. He looked at her with a little smile, and she talked to him and caressed his face. Culbert watched all this with tears glistening in his eyes and told me how things would change for his family. Both parents went back to the quiet room, and I left them talking quietly together.

I returned with some coffee for them, which they accepted gratefully. I sensed a change in the atmosphere as well as in their attitude toward each other. When they finished their coffee, we joined hands. I said a prayer for all of them and especially for Jeremy and Emma.

"Well, Marta, this has been quite a night. It's almost morning. I'll take you home. The car is parked near the hospital. Thank you, chaplain, for all your help. God bless you and all the staff."

I followed them outside, where they walked, arm in arm, toward the car. I turned toward the east and noticed the sky tinged a delicate shade of rose behind the dark trees, a promise of a beautiful day. That light reminded me of the verse in Isaiah 60:1, "Arise, shine, for thy Light has come." As I looked toward the faraway couple, I realized that, throughout that night, God was in control and he always would be. That bodes well for the future because he is a God of hope, one in whom we can put our trust.

Reflections on My Call

This morning is beautiful. An aura of freshness comes from the garden, and a breeze stirs the trees. Lilacs give off a lovely scent. It is refreshing to sit comfortably in my favorite chair and pray and muse about my life. I dreamed for many years of having a garden like this. I breathe in the gentle aromas from the flowers and delight in the soothing sound of water trickling into the pond that my son-in-law made for us. It is an oasis of colors, scents, and peace where I can immerse myself and let my mind wander.

I think about my past, the many experiences I've gone through, the people I've met who have been influential in my life, and my children, too. I'm retired now, but there was a time when my whole life lay before me and I had to decide what to do with it. My decision to be a chaplain had filled me with immense peace. I knew where I was going, and it felt like I was in the right place.

I think back to one night in 1986 at the Hospital for Sick Children in Toronto, where I sat by a little girl's bedside. Because of her unstable nervous condition, it had taken a while for Miriam to go to sleep, but now she slept peacefully. I watched her. Her mother had cried as she told me all the difficulties she had gone through with her three-year-old daughter. Earlier in the evening, when the nurse was checking on Miriam, I sat and listened to the mother, comforted her, and prayed with her. I promised her that I would sit by Miriam until she fell asleep. The mother could go home knowing her daughter was not alone.

All was quiet, except for the breathing of the sleeping children in the quiet ward and the occasional rustling of the nurses' uniforms as they went from bed to bed and checked on their patients. At peace, I relaxed in my chair. I didn't have to leave the hospital yet, so I rested. I thought back to the sad mother who was so broken at leaving her little girl behind.

Suddenly, it came to me. I wanted to do this for the rest of my life, to give comfort, reassurance, and support to those people who walk through suffering and pain. I would pray with them so they wouldn't feel alone through it all. I wanted to be a barrier to despair, confusion, and loneliness.

In those moments, I prayed that the Lord might help me to prepare carefully and diligently for this ministry. I remember the joy in my heart that I had found my call in life. The message had come with such clarity and strength, and it was especially for something I loved to do. I would dedicate my life to this calling.

Long years of preparation followed, including a degree and field placements, but all that preparation time never deterred me from my call. I was finally academically ready and began my spiritual journey as chaplain in several hospitals, following the call of my Lord. And he has blessed me all the time with his presence and security.

Of all the people I've had the opportunity to help, the children have touched my heart the most. Even in their suffering, they remained children, enjoying moments of laughter, play, and fun. They expressed their thankfulness with unblemished sincerity and love. Their innocence was perhaps their greatest defense against sickness. There were times, though they were suffering, when the illness seemed to affect the adults around them more. The children were always ready to talk about Jesus with a big smile and an unbridled curiosity.

My mind returns to the garden around me. A beautiful, bright cardinal comes near my window. The scents are still flowing and refreshing me. The Lord gives me beautiful, rewarding sights, sounds, and smells in my garden, as if to compensate for years of hard, tiring work. I believe my garden is God's gift to reward my family and me for years of faithful service to him.

Chapter 2

Like Sheep without a Shepherd

As I worked in one hospital after another to follow my call, I often met people who did not know what to do with their lives. Their sense of direction and purpose was confused. As a spiritual guide, I would remind them that great love and direction waited for them. I told them that God accepts everyone, meets them where they are in their life, and leads them gently. Most of the time, patients accepted that gentle nudge. In this chapter, I'll share several stories that illustrate God's intervention in their lives.

At times, we don't put enough value on the strength of our actions or words toward the betterment of others. As a chaplain, I often left situations wondering if I had helped at all. Had I brought anything to them that was special, healing, or helpful? Had I made a difference? Had I been God's emissary? I strove to apply 100 percent of my skill, yet I had inevitable moments of pause when I wondered about its effectiveness.

Many times, I received a pleasant look, a smile, or a kind word, and my whole day would instantly be transformed into one filled with joy. It may be that the same thing happens to someone I visit with unexpected results.

The Power of Prayer

I sometimes perceive a flicker of doubt within myself. I then truly admit I do not know God fully or perhaps I do not trust his full insight. Most often, my faith wavers when I pray for a very long time for something good to happen in someone's life and it does not happen.

For months, I prayed for a young patient at BGH to be healed. I pushed her to keep going as best she could and to focus on a brighter future when she would be better. I prayed and prayed for her to be well so she could enjoy a normal life, revel in the company of her friends, and be comforted.

It seemed she could not keep going. Regretfully, she passed away. Admittedly, she did not take good care of herself and wished to die. I wondered why. I had faith that God would intervene in her life and restore her health, but also come nearer to her spirit and lift it up. I realized that only God can explain why things happen the way they do. Perhaps he took her to himself to stop her suffering, her miserable loneliness, and her terrible insecurity, but still I found it difficult to say with belief, "Thy will be done."

I heard a report on the radio stating that, contrary to popular opinion, prayer has no benefit for people requiring medical care. Rather, it increases their levels of stress and anxiety. There were many responses to that controversy, so I can add mine. In some cases, when patients pray specifically to be rid of an illness, that outcome may not materialize. However, in every case, there is always the possibility of patients finding peace deep within themselves, knowing their pain and sorrows are borne by a power greater than the doctors and nurses and greater than themselves. In my work, I have experienced many different attitudes toward prayer. I firmly believe in the value of prayer. In my talk about spiritual care, I always stress the point that we are not fully capable of understanding its power.

One patient was very pleasant, but professed to be a stalwart atheist. Nonetheless, we were still able to carry on a cheerful conversation as to why he did not believe and why I did. He had proof that God did not exist, and nobody could change his mind. When I left him, I said, "Well, I will pray for you all the same, so you may enjoy peace in your soul, even though you do not believe in prayer."

"You do so, my dear. I will be very grateful that someone thinks of me. Prayer never hurts anybody."

"That is true. However, I have experienced times with people when prayer was actually beneficial."

One lady, Mary, was facing serious surgery, the amputation of her leg. Her nurse called me because they had prepped her for surgery. Mary was agitated and could not calm down. One of her children had tried everything to soothe her, but Mary was still deeply disturbed. So I sat by Mary's bed, and she told me how afraid she was of losing her leg. We examined why she was afraid. How could she manage at home? What about the pain? What if she did not heal well?

Her son assured her that everything would be ready at his own house and Mary could live with them as long as necessary. I assured

Mary that, in the hospital, they had medication strong enough to take the pain away and make her more comfortable.

Then I added, "You know, Mary, we can talk to someone who can give you better answers to all your questions and calm your fears. Would you let me pray to God with you and your children that you may be at peace for your surgery?"

"Oh, yes. We always need prayers," she answered vaguely.

So I took her in my arms and prayed for her to be at peace, for the doctors and nurses to call upon their skills and look after her, and for her children to be able to comfort and help her after her surgery. She cried. Then, exhausted, she lay back on her bed and closed her eyes. After a while, I left, assuring them I would be back after her surgery.

The next day, her nurse met me in the hall as I was going to visit Mary again. "You know, Mirella, after you left, Mary fell asleep for a few hours. When we took her to surgery, she was calm and even smiling. She said she knew things were in God's hands."

Mary made an amazing recovery, went to her son's home for a while, and kept in touch with me. I was always glad to hear her tell me she was doing quite well. I thought deeply how blessed this woman was in spite of her disease and the risks associated with major surgery. It affirmed my belief that the Lord blesses us abundantly, despite our miseries and difficulties. All we have to do is give our anxieties and fears over to him. We may not always heal the way we would like, even when we pray for it, but, through prayer, we do receive strength from God to cope with our pain and carry on, one day at a time.

It may be an overly simplified point of view for people who give statistics about the inefficiency of prayer, but I have seen many episodes where I prayed with a patient for realistic hope, a good night of sleep, trust in the doctor, good medication, and a smile. Then the next day, I would receive a positive report of peace and calm in that person.

I always tell the people I pray with that God is present at their side, bears their pain, and helps them to carry on one day at a time because he loves them infinitely. They are his great concern, and he never leaves them to struggle alone.

Prayer is the most intimate communication with our heavenly friend. When we pray with gratitude and calmness, it's as if we are leaning against God's breast, hearing his heart beating for us. We close our eyes and feel his arms around us. It is a state of absolute tranquility for our spirit.

Prayer is the most profound intimacy we may have with any being. God reveals his complete understanding of us. He reassures us of his infinite love. All we have to do is remain still and absorb the peaceful blessing that is healing in itself.

Code Blue

As a chaplain, there is no limit to the seemingly little things I can do for my patients. I do not regard them as insignificant. The care I provide is more qualitative than quantitative. I go deeper than merely understanding them as patients; I try to know them as the unique individuals they are.

One day, I was visiting with a patient who told me how he served the Lord for many years in his church. He was concerned about his illness and his long stay in the hospital, but he felt at peace. He was waiting for that time when he would go to the Lord.

An aura of peacefulness surrounded this white-haired gentleman as he sat near the window. Greeting cards and pictures of his family encircled him. A vase with flowers from his wife stood on a nearby table. A colorful afghan covered his bed. All these things contributed to the warm, cozy, and peaceful atmosphere where he sat contentedly and reminisced with me.

Suddenly, the announcement of a Code Blue interrupted our conversation. I took my time to pray with him and then hurried to the intensive care unit (ICU). When there is an announcement for a code, especially a Code Blue, the adrenaline starts to pump.

An aura of tension filled the hall. Someone had suffered a cardiac arrest. The trauma team literally flew to the scene where the red light flashed, as well as the additional people associated with such an emergency. I joined them, but was careful to stay out of the way. As a chaplain, it's important to answer such calls, to be there as needed for the patients and families involved.

In this case, a very large man in his fifties was brought in early that morning. Members of his family—natives from a nearby reserve—had found him unconscious on the bathroom floor. The staff had revived him, but now he was unconscious again. A battery of machines surrounded him and transmitted vital information. A team of doctors shouted orders, and the nurses obeyed. Everybody seemed to know what to do. They worked together and struggled to get a response, to bring back a pulse and save the life of this man.

I joined the family in the waiting room outside the unit, assuring them that the medical team was doing everything it could for their loved one. During that anxious waiting time, they asked me to pray for him, and, all together, we did. Then we waited and spoke only sporadically. I learned the patient's family was a close-knit one. Some spoke of God and prayed silently.

The doctor came in. He looked exhausted and sad. We knew the patient had not survived. The doctor explained what had happened. He tried to be clear and easy to understand. He had compassion in him. When he left, everybody sat stunned for a while. Some people started to cry; others sat immobile.

I asked what they would like to do. They expressed their wish to go and see him and later have a short committal service by his bed in the afternoon perhaps. I arranged for this to happen and accompanied them to the room where the patient lay. The air was still. An aura of respect and sadness was in the room as the family surrounded the bed. They spoke to the man, their brother and son, as though he were merely asleep. I stepped out of the room and left them to their good-byes. I silently closed the door.

A short time later, I went back for a short service by the bedside. I sensed that the family felt better. Though many people insist on calling a priest or their pastor, this family welcomed me and showed me great respect. The nurses had done an excellent job of getting this patient ready and cleared his room of all the medical equipment that had seemed so necessary earlier that day.

As before, family members gathered around the bed and held hands. I stood at the foot of the bed. Taking my time, I read Psalm 23:

The Lord is my shepherd, I shall not want.
He makes me lie down in green pastures,
He leads me beside quiet waters,
He restores my soul.
He guides me in paths of righteousness
For his name sake.
Even though I Walk through the valley of the shadow of death,
I will fear no evil, for you are with me;
Your road and your staff, they comfort me.
You prepare a table before me
In the presence of my enemies.
You anoint my head with oil;
My cup overflows.

Surely goodness and love will follow me
All the days of my life,
And I will dwell in the house of the Lord forever. (NIV)

Some of the people whispered the words with me. Then I talked briefly about death and how they needn't be afraid, but should rejoice because their loved one was face to face with Jesus and now knew all those things that were impossible for us to know. I talked about the eternal life that awaited all of us when we followed Jesus while we were on earth. I talked about the promise of Jesus to take us with him to his house of many mansions. I read John 14 in which Jesus states this promise.

Do not let your hearts be troubled. Trust in God; trust also in me. In my Father's house are many rooms ;if it were not so I would have told you. I am going to prepare a place for you.
(NIV)

I finally concluded with a prayer of thanksgiving for this family's loved one and asked them to receive God's blessing. We closed with the Lord's Prayer. As I gave out some pamphlets about grief, I noticed that, even through their tears, they seemed peaceful and composed.

The memory of that service has always remained vivid for me. I had performed many ceremonies in the same way, and people responded with gratitude and respect. It gave me peace to know I helped to bring someone closer to the Lord and to his promises.

The Human Touch

While on my rounds one day, I stopped at the threshold of a patient's room. Inside, a lady was struggling with bone cancer. The sight of her filled me with great compassion because she appeared to be in much pain and discomfort. She sat up in her bed, in what seemed to be an uncomfortable position, and struggled to hold her neck up despite the brace she wore to support it. I entered the room, approached her bed, and placed my hand on her forehead. I pronounced a short blessing.

Her eyes were closed, but she said, "Oh, the touch of a human hand. How refreshing!" She looked at me and smiled. "I should have known it was you, chaplain. Would you pray with me?"

I prayed with her and talked with her for a while. She told me that she had been placed in isolation. She had Methicillin-resistant Staphylococcus aureus (MRSA), a particularly nasty "superbug" that is resistant to all forms of penicillin. I hadn't noticed the sign at the entrance to her room when I first went to her. Probably very few people had touched her. If they had, they used gloves. I realized then that I should not have touched her, but perhaps my touch had brought comfort and encouragement to her. Despite the risk to my health, I did not regret it.

Of course, when I visited her again, I wore gloves, but, that day, she taught me that simple physical contact between humans produces positive results, perhaps more than words could convey. What people can teach me, even in sickness and helplessness, always moves me. She had been so appreciative of what I thought were simple actions. To her, it was a ministry of presence, and it humbled me that my touch had brought so much meaning.

A Little Angel

These days, it is all too easy to become discouraged at the state of the world. Nonetheless, while ministering in the hospitals, I witnessed many acts of compassion that made me optimistic about the fate of humankind. If we watch for these moments of kindness, they can fill our hearts with hope.

A patient on one of the floors was nearing the end of his life. A bank of machines surrounded him, and many tubes connected him to them. His hair was a wild mass of gray. His face, unshaven for days, was a mass of stubble. He did not smell good, and he slept most of the time, but, when he opened his eyes, they were as wild as his hair. He seemed to have difficulty focusing on me and could utter only a few words. There was no way to really converse with him, but I stopped by his bed a few times. If he were awake, I said a short prayer for him. I think he heard me because he tried to smile.

When I arrived at his bedside one afternoon, he was asleep. The only sound was that of the gurgling tubes that sustained him, a heartbreaking sight indeed. I noticed he held a little silver angel in one hand.

When I left the room, one of the aides asked, "Did you notice the angel?"

"Yes, he has it in his hand, but I didn't want to wake him up to ask about it."

"Well, I went to the gift shop to get it for him. I always clean that room, and he does not have anybody to visit him. I don't think he's doing well, but he thanked me for the angel. I hope it gives him comfort."

"I'm sure it will. It was so thoughtful of you to do that for him. I also think he has few people who care for him. Thank you, my dear."

I continued to visit this man. He was sometimes awake or sometimes deeply asleep, but, whatever his state, he either held that angel in his hand or had it on the table beside him. He was eventually discharged, but I do not know if he went home or somewhere else. I hope he still has that little angel to give him comfort and the sense that someone watches over him.

That gesture from the aide moved me. She had shown compassion and care for another human being who was suffering. Such acts of compassion keep us going in our ministry because they make us realize we are not alone as we care for others.

As human beings, we all long to have someone do things for us, call us on the phone, and maybe even write us a little note. It's funny how those little acts make our lives so much more positive and hopeful. When we wait for them to occur and they don't, we feel dejected. Understanding this need makes us more aware of the need to bestow acts of kindness on our neighbors—actions, no matter how small they are—that make a difference to those who walk through life alone.

The "Christ's Woman"

A chaplain has a variety of titles, depending on how an individual feels toward the person who comes to visit in the name of God. People have addressed me as Father, Padre, Sister, Reverend, Minister, and Chaplain. While all of these titles are quite acceptable, I always preferred to be called by my first name, Mirella. It made me feel more down-to-earth, more like a friend than a stranger.

However, one title took me quite aback. One day, I visited a patient named Jim, who had been diagnosed with cirrhosis of the liver. He received me with an air of neutrality, neither accepting me as a God's messenger but not rejecting my presence altogether. He knew I was the chaplain, but he preferred to restrict his conversation to non-religious topics. I went along with him and offered my full attention and listening ear.

When I came back a few days later, he was sitting in the hall where the sun was pouring in through the windows. Family and friends surrounded him. I approached the group just to say hello and be on my way. Because he was having a visit with his family, I did not wish to disturb them.

However, he saw me and smiled. "Oh, this is … This is … I can't remember your name. This is the Christ's woman. Very nice of you to come and see how I'm doing."

For a while, I didn't know what to say. People nodded and smiled at me in a friendly way.

"Well, I'm really the chaplain in this hospital, and I talk about our Lord Jesus Christ to people like Jim. I will come again, Jim, and talk to you about whatever you like. It's very nice to meet your family today."

Some people continued their conversations, so I said good-bye and let him continue with his visit. The title he used had stunned me. Even in his sickness, he had been able to understand my ministry. He had perceived that I would have liked to talk to him about Christ, but I was waiting for a signal of acceptance and participation from him. Incidentally, the next day, I was able to direct his thoughts toward Christ and found he had a shy faith, hidden by years of indifference and alcoholism.

The title he gave me, "Christ's woman," humbled me. That's what I am, and that's what everybody is, but are we really? At times, I feel I take my ministry and whom I represent—Christ on earth—in a very light way. I don't go deeply into a conversation for fear of imposing, as in Jim's case, but do I have the right to do so? What would Christ do in my case?

I humbly submit to the fact that I'm not Christ. We only bring his name forward in our lives and the lives of others. And I hope that sometimes, through our imperfect attempts, God can bring out that goodness.

Renewed

In times of sickness, loss, and tragedy, it is instinctive for our mind and soul to seek out a power that is superior to any here on earth. A search begins within the depths of our being for what one believes. From a young age, many of us have been instilled with certain beliefs, values, and fundamental questions about life and our existence that we carry around for many years. During a crisis, such as an illness, those beliefs often surface and make us look at life from a different perspective. The foundations, practices, and rituals of a religious life that we were exposed to as children may have been forgotten and pushed deep down inside our souls, far away from our consciousness, but now they resurface, making us aware that there is more to life.

Unsurprisingly, at such a time, I receive calls from people who, to put it simply, wish to put their spiritual affairs in order as they deal with the onset of a serious disease. A nurse called me one morning and explained his patient was deeply disturbed. Perhaps a talk with me would help him relax. Paul, a young man with HIV, was admitted to the hospital to take care of several problems due to his run-down condition.

The first thing he told me was that he wanted to do "confession," but thought it was too late for him. I, sensing this conversation might take a while, pulled up a chair. "All right. Let's first examine why it's too late."

He turned off the radio and sat a little higher in the bed to focus on me. "I was brought up Catholic. I even served as an altar boy. Then I got into a lot of things I'm not proud of and got sick. I had blood transfusions that gave me HIV. I left the church for many years and don't know how to start again to go to it."

"Can you tell me what confession means to you?"

"Well, I was reading the gospel where it says Jesus was crucified with two criminals. And one of them asked Jesus to be forgiven. Did he have to wait to be forgiven?" he asked me in a trembling voice.

"I can tell you what I know of Jesus. He forgives everyone the instant he or she asks him because he has told us so. He does that because he loves us and wants us to be acceptable in God's sight. All you have to do, Paul, is to ask God to forgive you for the things you have done in the past, and he will."

"How will I know that he has forgiven me?"

"First of all, he has said so many times in the Bible, and we believe his word is true. Second, you will feel at peace with yourself and others and will not be afraid of your disease."

"I have started to ask him many times, but I've never felt that peace. You can't hear my confession, right? I will need a priest."

"I can hear your confession, but the Lord Jesus forgives you. If it makes you feel more comfortable, I can arrange for a priest to come to see you."

"Oh, yes, could you do that? I would be very grateful."

The next day, I arranged for one of our priests who visited the hospital regularly to see Paul. Father Don sought me out afterward and told me more about Paul's situation and how he had accepted God's forgiveness with joy. Father Don had talked at length with Paul about his life.

During the next week, I tried to see Paul several times, but he was either asleep or out of his room. Soon after, he was discharged and went back to his family. His nurse told me what a different man he was when he left the hospital and said I made the change in him, but I knew who was really responsible for Paul's transformation. Paul was happy and hopeful. He felt much better and walked tall. I knew it was all due to God's intervention in his life. Paul received God's forgiveness and felt the "peace that passes understanding" finally settling in his heart.

The Christian Jew

One night, I was on call at one of Toronto Hospitals
. I had just settled for the night, and I was in that stage of slumber where sleep is overcoming all imagination and wakefulness. Suddenly, my pager went off and rudely jarred me back to reality. The call had come from a far wing of the hospital. I dressed quickly while trying to clear my head from the buzzing of sleep that, moments before, had nearly overcome me.

When I reached the patient, I saw he was an older man with curly white hair. He sat up in bed and peeled an apple with one small light on. The patient in the bed beside him was snoring peacefully on the other side of the curtain. As I approached, he smiled and invited me to sit down.

"Well, Sister, sorry to call you so late, but I couldn't sleep. Something is bothering me, and I wonder if you can help me. Would you think I'm crazy if I told you I am a Jew, born and raised, and saw Jesus standing by my bed the other night? I haven't had any peace ever since. What does it mean?"

I had to gather my thoughts before answering such a heavy question in the middle of the night when all I wanted to do was sleep. He had disturbed me for this? Could he not have waited until morning? In my selfishness, I got ready to have a conversation about it. Then I realized I was on call to answer for my Lord. So I settled quietly to listen.

"I don't think you are crazy. Many people have seen Jesus in their lives and interpreted it one way or another as their conscience told them. In your case, perhaps Jesus wants to tell you something you need to know."

He offered me a piece of his apple. For a moment, we munched away and felt comfortable with each other.

"Well, you're right, Sister. I have known Jesus with all the other prophets all my life. You know what I think? He wants to be my friend. Do you think it's crazy?"

I smiled at this man's childlike wonderment. "No, sir, it isn't crazy at all. What I can tell you is what I firmly believe. Jesus wants and seeks to be a friend of all who need and accept him. Perhaps you need him as a friend in your life at the moment. In your imagination, you have turned to the best person you know who could be such a friend. Actually, you are very blessed. If you accept him, he will pour all kinds of blessings on you."

"What shall I have to do then?" he inquired eagerly and leaned toward me.

"I think you just need to be still and accept him in your heart. Tell him so, and wait for his peace to come over you."

"Years ago, I was in a very sad situation, in despair and feeling frustrated with myself and others. In my mind, I clung to the foot of the cross and stayed there, quietly waiting. After a while, I went about my business and felt nothing was different. But it was, and I realized it after a good night's sleep because peace flooded over me. My life has been so much more serene and content. I had found such a friend, the best friend I ever had, even though I couldn't see him. I felt him walk beside me from then on. I wish you could experience something like that."

Long into the night, we talked about Jesus, his life, his miracles, and what it meant to follow him. The man displayed a good knowledge of history and the New Testament. He grew more interested and excited as time went on. He was smiling, and tears were in his eyes.

"I'm tired now. But I think I will find him as my best friend eventually. Your words are so beautiful and comforting. I'm glad I called you. I think I'll sleep better tonight. Thank you for sharing Jesus with me. I think I'm going to love him and continue to be a cultural Jew with Jesus in my heart." He laughed and shook my hand.

As I reached my room that night, I felt excited. What I always wanted to do had happened, to show Jesus and his love to someone who needed it. I prayed for the Jewish gentleman that he would find peace that night and walk with Jesus. I also hoped he would have the courage to hold onto him in the midst of his culture and congregation.

I realized sleep was gone for me that night with all the excitement and reflections, but then I had been on call for God to one of his needy children. What was one sleepless night for me, compared to God's tremendous love for us?

The People in Blue Smocks

The world is full of people who, regardless of their faith or religious beliefs, make it their responsibility to do good things for others, performing acts of charity, displaying outstanding generosity, and conveying loving thoughts that may often go unnoticed.

The people in the blue smocks, whom you see in hospital waiting rooms and corridors, are like those people mentioned above. You can't miss them. However, these volunteers take on many tasks that go above and beyond their job description. They work in all departments and medical units. They are usually smiling and well groomed. And they are so very kind. Their words and actions may change a person's day from dark into sunny and may convert despair into hope. Why do they do it?

One volunteer said, "It's in me to volunteer, to help others. My mother volunteered for everything. She helped many causes through her life, and I'm the same. I think Jesus made the supreme sacrifice for me on the cross, so this is just a little I can do for him."

After retiring, I decided to volunteer, too, in the same building with which I was so familiar and the people I'd come to know. When I see people struggling to get things done, I can't just pass by and watch with pity. I feel compelled to lend a hand in every possible way—physical, financial, spiritual, and emotional—because, in the end, I know it returns lovingly to my Lord.

I asked some of my fellow volunteers why they came to the hospital every week. Between laughs, a man said, "I come for the free coffee and doughnuts."

Another man said, "Oh, I come to see the beautiful women."

We all laughed with him. What a wonderful moment we enjoyed, sitting in the lounge together before going to our posts and enjoying a friendly conversation.

One of the older ladies said, "I like to come here twice a week because it gives me something worthwhile to do with my time. After working all your life, you get used to being busy with yourself."

Another lady smiled approvingly. "It feels good to help someone who is in need. What if I were in that situation? I'd really like to have someone help me and be with me."

Certain volunteers bring patients down to the worship service in the chapel every week. They have to walk up several floors and do a lot of transporting, but they do it cheerfully, and it gives them great pleasure to see the chapel filled with people singing and praying together.

The volunteers sit with the patients in the chapel and help them through the service. Then they take them back to their rooms when the service is over. At times, the volunteers don't feel well themselves, but they continue with their tasks, smiling and encouraging everybody. The manager of volunteers, who is always ready to give a hand and encourage both patients and other volunteers with positive comments, runs the whole department smoothly, efficiently, and on a cheerful note. Clearly, the generosity of our volunteers greatly benefits everyone in the hospital benefits

The journey of a volunteer

Spring was in the air, and the sky was a perfect blue. As I wandered around BGH, I felt elated that another winter had passed and spring would soon be here. Then a call came to see a patient, and I hurried to meet this person with a fervent prayer that I could be of help, whatever the situation might be.

A young woman greeted me with a smile. Sunlight flooded the room, and all of the patients in the four-bed unit had flowers next to their beds, but the one who had called for me had her leg in traction and appeared uncomfortable.

"You're the chaplain, I guess," she said pleasantly. "My name is Barbara. It's been many months already, and I'm still here. I'd like to tell you my story. I know you're the person who hears many stories of sorrow and suffering. You must be a very special person to be able to bear all this without going crazy. I have been in and out of hospitals for the last eight months. It happened with a car accident and a minor fracture, and look at me now. They had to break my leg again because it wasn't healing properly. I'm not even sure it's going to be all right this time. I've had so many things go wrong for me. I'm not going to tell you about them. I just needed someone to cry with and feel sympathetic about me, so I called you." Tears streamed down her face as she finished talking.

"Barbara, I'm glad I'm here to listen to you. You can tell me all you want, and it will stay with me. There's another person who also listens when I'm not around and can give you comfort. Do you know who I'm talking about?" I dried her face with a tissue.

"Of course I know. You're talking about God. I go to church when I can and have been active in some of their activities at St. Basil's Church, like working with children. I'm a teacher when I'm well. Somehow, I didn't feel comfortable talking to God about my troubles all the time. He seems to be so far away from all of us while you're close to me. If you could sometimes come to visit me, it would really do me a lot of good."

I was alone in the pastoral care department, so I organized a network of pastoral visitors and volunteers who could help with visiting patients. In the following weeks, I visited Barbara a few times and occasionally sent a pastoral visitor to her.

During one of my visits, she took my hand and said, "You know, Mirella, I think I'm ready to talk to God with you. Will you stay with me while I pray?"

I took her hands in mine, and she prayed, "O God, you know me. I need your help to get well. Please forgive me for going far from you. Bless me in the name of the Father, the Son, and the Holy Spirit. Amen."

And I prayed with her. At the end, she smiled. "I believe things will go better with my leg this time."

I kept visiting her and praying with her until she was discharged for physiotherapy. Then one morning, I saw her coming down the corridor, walking with a cane and smiling.

"You know, things are much better now. I can walk again, and I'll soon go back to work. The best thing about this experience is that I have renewed my faith and my prayer life. Thank you for persevering with me."

Being retired doesn't mean that I stop listening to God. I still hear and obey the quiet voice that urges me to help, so I'm a volunteer at BGH. It was my great joy to learn that Barbara is a volunteer now, too. She serves others with great pleasure because she says we receive so much from other people that, when we can, it's a delight to give back a part of what we have received. It's a great lesson to learn, and, when we do, we are so much richer for it. I can certainly attest to that.

I am reminded of the generosity and kindness of people at BGH and how much I enjoyed working with the people there. From the aides to managers, they have all affected me with their thoughtfulness and gentleness. In the hustle and bustle of our busy lives, it's easy to overlook these small kindnesses, but, when I stop and take time to look for them, I find the love and input of such people enriches lives and makes me able to continue our work the next day.

Patients may not be aware of it, but they contribute to the care of others. In numerous instances, I learned something from a visit with one patient that was applicable to the situation of another patient facing a similar situation.

Care for the Caregivers

Nurses, doctors, and therapists walk through the hospital with great efficiency and professionalism. Yet, at times, they are sure to experience moments of weakness and discouragement. They may feel alone in their work or may feel nobody cares about them. Times of personal trouble affect them and may hinder their performance. In such a time, staff would come to me with their problems and for spiritual guidance and comfort.

When counseling staff, I keep in mind the many things I learned from my mother about hospital life. Having been a nurse before she married my father, she dedicated herself to raising her children and did not have to balance a career with family as some of her peers did.

My mother told us stories from her nursing experience in a hospital in North Italy that the Protestant nuns of the Waldensian Order ran. I listened as she recounted the nonchalance of surgeons in the operating room, who went about their tasks while whistling or singing. I found those stories fascinating.

On winter mornings, my mother and her friends huddled around the radiator for some warmth in those long, cold corridors, and they tried to steal a few more minutes of sleep before starting their duties.

My mother's tales included knowledge of many treatments and home remedies, which she still used on her family. From the stories, I learned about her strict discipline, the efficiency she put into all her tasks, and her devotion to her patients. She put in long hours of cleaning, making beds, administering medications, and redoing bandages. She loved her work and sometimes said that, if she had not had her family to raise, she would have gone back to nursing and had more training. In my work with patients, I have encountered their nurses, and many have shown their dedication and diligent care that went beyond their duty, just as my mother must have done.

When I went to the maternity floor at BGH, I often found a group of nurses sitting together, each one holding a baby and rocking. Such loving care and sense of serenity surrounded those babies in the first days of their lives.

At the Sick Children's Hospital in Toronto, the nurses often sat by the patients' beds, gently urging a child to go to sleep or coaxing a child with little games and laughter to take medication that was so important to getting better. Those actions spoke of a dedication beyond duty.

I have also watched nurses as they worked with oncology patients. On treatment days, the nurses did whatever they could to make patients comfortable, like talking cheerfully while inserting needles for the intravenous treatment. The nurses also told me why a patient was not there that day, especially if there had been a death. They also encouraged me to talk to anyone who looked dejected and sick, affirming the importance of my spiritual assistance to them.

In the palliative care clinic at St. Joseph's, Brantford, the nurses were trained to deal with people nearing the end of life. Many nurses dedicated long hours to the care of those special patients. We often experienced a time when many patients died. Some were still young, in their thirties or forties. In such a situation, it was very difficult for the nurses. It affected them at the core of their being.

We hosted several briefing sessions and allowed all staff from the unit to vent their feelings over all those young deaths. Then we helped them to learn ways of coping with it. Encouraged in their work, they would go back to their stations, affirmed they had done everything possible to help those patients so they could go on.

In the ER at BGH, I had the opportunity to experience nursing care personally. When I arrived with shortness of breath, the medical staff took care of me quickly and efficiently. I was amazed at how one of the nurses checked on me, encouraging me and letting me know that the doctor would come soon. As I waited, I saw that same nurse check on others with the same cheerful and gentle attitude, asking them how they felt, if they wanted a drink, or if they wanted her to call their family. She sometimes gave them a back rub. I experienced and witnessed quality of care at its highest level in a busy ward.

Back in my office, staff came to me with their personal problems. They could have gone to a professional agency, but they preferred to come and talk with me first. We examined the problem, and I would invite them to see a possible solution or better angle. They often asked for prayer for patience, understanding, and courage. Afterward, they told me how much lighter they felt after unburdening.

It made me feel good to be able to help them, listen to their troubles, and show compassion and understanding of their life and duties. I knew their tasks were very demanding at times and some patients did not respond to them in a positive way. Yet, I could see both sides of the story, too, and realize there might have been a lack of patience and understanding on both sides.

Working close to the staff in many departments, brought me many new friendships. I enjoyed and valued those people because they made my work easier and more pleasant. Even now as a volunteer, I still enjoy friendly talks with the staff. I have been blessed by so many encouraging and supporting staff members, especially by their dedication to their calling, which helps make BGH the excellent facility it is today.

Chapter 3

They Shall Blossom Even in Their Old Age

Ministering to elderly people was something of an epiphany for me. It meant working with a group of people with whom I had previously paid little attention. Prior to my training, I had only occasional contact with them, and it was always in social contexts. None of which offered any special insight or understanding about life at an advanced age. Now I was meeting them every day as their spiritual caregiver, and I realized the need of special skills for my ministry with them.

My work brought me to the many places where elderly people lived. Each place required a different type of ministry, so these reflections vary in their focus and tone. However, all my encounters instilled and broadened a great sense of compassion for them. I applied myself to be more attentive and helpful to them.

The inspiration for this chapter came while I was vacationing one summer in Algonquin Park. The lush greenery of the trees, surrounding vegetation, and the calmness of its many lakes instilled a deep serenity in my soul, from which my thoughts flowed easily.

My husband Ernest and I set out on a long hike in the park one day. The trail went uphill and down and then veered off to the side, basically every which way but straight. The path was extremely rugged. Stones and tree roots formed the road we followed. Trees of all varieties towered everywhere. In some places, small bridges and rustic staircases made the climbing and the descending a bit easier. We reached the top of the hill and sat on its brow to rest and reflect. Completely drenched in perspiration, but elated to have walked this difficult path for two solid hours, I felt extremely well, yet somewhat tired and hungry. I drank in the captivating sight of a small lake below, where two beaver lodges had been built. We spotted blue herons, turtles, and delicate water lilies floating on the water below. It was a sight of utter peace and tranquility, a fitting reward after a long walk.

Then I saw a stand of trees nearby. Tall and thin, they stretched straight toward the sky. Ernest pointed out that they were young trees and lucky to have survived the fierce storm that had passed through the day before. Looking closer, I spotted an older tree, gnarled and partly uprooted. It leaned against the young trunks. How it was still standing was a wonder. The older tree looked as if it were leaning against the younger trees for support, taking whatever nourishment it could from the ground where some roots were still anchored. At the same time, the young trees received protection from the hot sun, growing strong in the shade of the lone older one. The sun bathed everything there, and birds flew around them and hovered over the trees.

I said aloud to my husband how that scene was like people. As a younger generation of people supports their elder generation, so, too, do the aged population offer protection and shelter with their knowledge and wisdom. That is our situation in life. Both the young and old need each other, as shown by those trees I saw that day.

When people reach old age, they face many changes. Their diet may be different because they can no longer shop for their own food or prepare it as they used to. Their independence is curbed because of the continuous care and coming and going of their caregivers. Perhaps they can no longer get out and about by themselves. They likely feel very lonely at times, perhaps even bitter, when their family doesn't seem to care for them as before, only offering the occasional phone call. A lower income may cause added financial stress when paying the bills, and obtaining expensive medications is harder than it used to be. Seniors may feel they are being treated like children because their senses have been dulled over the years, and they do not react to sounds and sights as they once did.

For a caregiver, it takes a great deal of understanding, patience, and tolerance to live with and care for an older person. Many functions, which are so easily and quickly accomplished for younger people, take a long time for the elderly person to perform.

Being independent almost becomes a fight for life. To be able to walk on one's own, not depending on a wheelchair or a walker to get around, is a sign of independence. Some elderly people can't walk far, yet they struggle to stand by themselves and walk as much as they can every day. It's a great strain, but they try to overcome their challenges at any cost, showing they still have some control.

Something that always makes me sad is witnessing the agony of many elderly people when they lose their sight and hearing. They struggle with all the faculties left to them to hear what is being said. They turn on bright lights to see the person who is talking to them, and they get frustrated with helpful devices such as hearingaids. It's just not the same as when they were younger. We may see people just sitting there, as if they are staring into space. Memories of past days when they felt stronger and more capable may be all that is left to them.

I watch elderly people going through their physiotherapy sessions after a stroke, a fracture, or surgery. They cry in pain, helplessness, and frustration, even though the therapist is there trying to help. We laugh and rejoice at a child's helplessness as he learns to walk and watch with trepidation and jubilation as he takes the first tentative steps, but we agonize with the elderly person for each painful step he or she is able to take.

I spent many years ministering to older seniors. Each individual's circumstances have been unique, but some needs were common to all of them: patience, sensitivity, and, above all, compassion.

Working with Psychiatric Patients

When I started working at Whitby Psychiatric Hospital, it was made up of several cottages, each one housing patients with a particular mental illness. Thus we had separate cottages (and schools) for adolescent, geriatric, and neuropsychiatric patients. As well, there were buildings for medical treatment and pastoral care. Each cottage had its own atmosphere, and it was specially designed to cater to the needs of the patients living in that building. Now the hospital is just one large building that houses all the patients.

I was a student in the Clinical Pastoral Education (CPE) unit. Being new there, I was anxious. Would I be able to work with these patients? The supervisor led our class on a small tour of the hospital, introducing us to the wards that we would visit during our training. I eventually became quite comfortable with my environment. When my training was finished, I stayed there for a while as an assistant chaplain. I later spent my internship there when I was preparing for ordination.

One of the first things I noticed during my training is that patients were always ready to talk about God, but not about Jesus Christ. Perhaps talking about Christ presupposes a commitment, a personal note of knowledge and faith. And perhaps patients were not ready to commit themselves to Christ because their hallucinations, confusion, and struggles made their lives so difficult. What would happen if they accepted Christ? Might they fear what he can do for them? Was it too big a commitment?

Each time I preached in the chapel, I felt sure I wanted to present to my listeners the Christ I knew, someone who was real, alive, and vibrant and of whom there was no need to be afraid. In all my sermons, I presented Jesus in his different aspects, as shepherd, teacher, healer, miracle worker, friend, and Savior. I felt a deep sense of satisfaction about this because, deep inside, I knew this was what he wanted me to do: present him in simple words to people in great need of his love.

Kelsey says in his book *Caring*, "Our capacity to love reaches its full when we can look upon the twisted features of a fellow being in pain and not turn away in fear and disgust, but catch a glimpse of the face of the suffering Christ and minister to him in all simplicity and tenderness."[1]

Little by little, just as Kelsey wrote, I allowed my compassion to flow out to these people, and my fear decreased. I got used to all the displays of abnormal behavior and could minister more diligently. Some patients reverently kissed my hand. I wondered what they felt in those moments. How much did they understand about me and my position among them?

I would like to think that they remembered me from one week to the next, but then I would see them later—lost in their own private world—where the most important thing was to have a cigarette. I spent time talking to some of them about their future and what they would do when they left the hospital. Then the next day, they'd do something so irrational that completely upset their lives and jeopardized their chances of getting out or surviving once they got out. I felt so incapable of helping them. They cried in despair, seeking help, and I didn't know how to give them what they so desperately needed.

At times, they looked at me expectantly, as if I possessed some powerful magic that would make them feel better right away. They seemed to think I could change their lives because I represented God. I felt compelled to talk to them, explain things, and try to find a solution to their problems, but I had to remember that I wasn't there to fix things, just to help them cope with the challenges of their illnesses.

Knowing I didn't have to make their problems go away brought great relief. I just had to listen. I couldn't fix their lives. They had to do that task for themselves with psychiatric help. I could stand by in faith and prayer. In every case, I prayed, "Forgive me, Lord, when

---

[1] Morton T. Kelsey, *Caring: How can we love one another* (Paulist Press, 1980), 181.

I have the task you have charged me with in my hands, I panic. Forgive my inadequacy and my fear that I lack competence in the task."

In these patients, I sense a tremendous struggle to break free from their sickness, the medication, and hospital life. They want to get out of the cycle of blaming everybody and everything for their misery and, most of all, accusing God of doing nothing to relieve their agony. I remember one middle-aged patient who thought like that. She had a troubling past, having attempted suicide on several occasions, which had brought her to the hospital. She had a youthful appearance, but a mournful look on her pretty face. Jean used to come to the chapel "to put things in order" for me. It seemed important for her to be in the chapel and chat with me.

One morning, she came to me looking more despondent than ever, so I invited her to go for a walk with me. We went outdoors and sat on a bench. She complained that everything was wrong, everybody was selfish, nobody did anything for her, and life was miserable.

I listened attentively and with compassion. Then I said, "Jean, look around you. There isn't so much wrong with this scenario, is there?"

She looked around. The grass was green, and the sun shone and reflected off the shimmering blue lake just beyond us. The flowers were in bloom. Even some geese were waddling by.

"Yes." She smiled and took a deep breath. The breeze played with her blonde curls. "I guess there is nothing wrong with the world, as you point it out." For a while, she took in the view and breathed in the fresh, scented air of the spring, but I'm not sure she was convinced.

"You see, Jean, God is always in control, even when we think he doesn't care. He does care. He wants us to enjoy his world and feel better just going for a walk and seeing what is around us. Try to see him around you."

And she did. She went for a long walk and then told me later how much better she felt. She was going to walk like that every day. It was the best tonic she had felt in some time.

There was something worthwhile in each resident, and the staff tried to do their best to help each person to develop to his or her potential. I also analyzed my feelings and strived to do my best for each individual that I met in this place because I believed Christ's atonement was also for them.

I noticed how the residents emerged from their cocoons—the protection they built around themselves—and how they cared for one another. I witnessed acts of great kindness between patients. They understood each other in their illness. They knew what the other was going through. They were kind to each other because everyone was carrying a burden. I saw an older man sit by a younger one. They talked companionably and went for a walk by the lake. They appeared to be good friends who cared for each other.

Seeking the Lord's Blessing

A woman requested a special service of blessing for her husband, a psycho-geriatric patient who was rapidly deteriorating. She wanted to ease the transition for him and the family. She felt guilty about having admitted him to the hospital and about not being able to visit him every day. She hadn't been able to cope with this sickness and didn't understand it very well. Their children felt that something terrible had happened in his brain to bring him to such a state of deterioration. They didn't think he would live much longer, and they were very supportive of their parents by being present and praying with them.

We gathered one Sunday afternoon in the lounge. An orderly wheeled the man into the room where we had gathered. I had prepared a simple service of devotion and invited the family to participate. All members of the family spoke in turn about their relationship with him. We prayed for the man. The family went away with heavy hearts, yet with a peaceful feeling that they had placed him totally in the Lord's hand at the service.

The Effect of Worship

Every Wednesday, we had a worship service in the chapel. Patients, staff, and volunteers attended. After the service, we enjoyed coffee and a visit in the lounge next door.

One evening soon afterward, one of the patients asked my supervisor, "How does it feel to be a Christian?"

My supervisor answered with one word, "Joyous."

That answer stunned me. How can anyone be joyous in a mental hospital? But I came to understand the depth of that answer. When we have a true faith in God, we rely on him, and our burdens become less heavy and more bearable. Like Jean, we look at the world around us, and we can still find it beautiful and good. We can accept many things in life, like disability or illness, and be content. With our faith, we build a sense of hope.

The chapel offered a place of refuge for many employees and patients. Many came to seek the chaplains just to talk for a while and be at rest. I often preached there on Sunday, and we always had a good-sized group. Many patients believed that attending church was part of their healing process. I spoke to them about the God who loves them, has compassion for them, and accepts them as they are. Inside, I cried for them, noticing how eagerly they listened to my words. I sometimes sang beautiful hymns of hope for them to refresh their spirit.

Working with the Seniors

By the beginning of my second year working at Whitby, I had taken my ordination vows with the Baptist Convention of Ontario and Quebec. After years of hard work and study, looking after my family, and working in my church and at the hospital, I felt proud of having finally reached my goal. My heart sang with joy.

One afternoon, my supervisor asked me to visit with a man in the geriatric department. The patient had requested a minister's visit and received me graciously. I felt quite elated for having received that call. We spent a good deal of time in conversation discussing his past, his church life, his family, and his job. When it came time for me to leave, the nurse came in to get him ready for his nap. He told her, "I had a nice conversation with this nice lady. I had asked for a minister, but they sent me this lady. Well, perhaps another time."

"Well," I thought, "there goes my pride at being an ordained minister. That's how it will be with many people. In their eyes, I'm not really a minister because I'm a woman."

After all, having woman clergy was still quite new to people, and some churches didn't accept women to such a ministry. It didn't bother me too much though, and I continued in my calling as if there had been no disappointment.

A young woman sat by her elderly mother, Martha, holding her hand and talking to her. Martha nodded in her chair, evidently not able to follow the conversation. When Martha's husband arrived, both he and his daughter helped Martha to get up, and together they walked with her in the garden outside. Every hesitant step the woman took was a victory. Her trembling and unsteady gait was a matter of great concern for her husband and daughter, but they continued to walk with her, assisting her lovingly. When they returned to the room, another ritual began, that of helping Martha eat her yogurt and fruit and carefully assisting her with every bite.

The daughter spoke to me one day about how difficult it was for them to see Martha deteriorate like that and how hard they had tried to help her function on a more normal level. Sometimes, they took her home for a visit, but it was becoming more difficult, and Martha slept most of the time. The daughter told me that she felt guilty, as if her mother's disease were partly her fault. So her anxiety was most palpable. The daughter felt comfortable talking with me because she had no one who would listen to her without judgment. She needed to talk, and I was very glad to offer her the support she needed.

Another woman sat clutching her bag and waiting for her husband in the living room. She told me how a stroke had incapacitated him and affected his brain. I asked her if she had family support. She said she didn't have any. Her children were busy with their lives and didn't understand their father's condition. I commented that she must feel the Lord at her side, and she agreed. Yes, the Lord was within her.

Her husband arrived, walking unsteadily and gazing vaguely about him. She looked at him with such love and took his face between her hands with great tenderness. She kissed him softly and murmured in German. I stepped back. I didn't want to disrupt their intimacy. I witnessed a love that set aside the illness (the dementia) and was only concerned with the welfare of the other.

Some of these patients had been married to their spouses for more than sixty years. When disease suddenly strikes one of them, the affected person, who is well known and loved, disappears, and the body is still there with all its demands and needs. Their partners still love him or her, but it is very painful to come and visit because there is little to no response. In most cases, the ill partner can't reciprocate any emotions.

There is such heartbreaking pain in seeing the awkward movements, hearing the noises the ill partner makes, and, for the one who is well, realizing the partner will never share the same bed, be at home for meals, or be there as a companion.

A woman cried when she related to me how her husband slapped her now and told her to go away. Before his illness, he would call her his little flower and take her in his arms and kiss her tenderly.

Another lady came every day on the bus from Toronto to be with her husband. When he saw her, he calmed down a little, and she would feed him. Otherwise, he wouldn't eat at all. While we were talking, he appeared completely naked before us. His wife screamed. I quickly grabbed a blanket, put it around him, and guided him to his room. A nurse came quickly to take him. Then I went back to his wife, who was crying disconsolately, and tried to comfort her.

"You have to think of him as a child now. He doesn't know what he's doing. So he feels like taking off his clothes and walking around. For him, it's all right. Think of him as a child of God. God loves him, even when he behaves this way. God does not blame him, and he is not ashamed of him. Try to accept this, my dear."

She readjusted the kerchief on her head, and together we went to his room. He waved at her and smiled, and I left them alone.

One afternoon, we were in the dining room attending a special party for the residents and their families. Everyone was having a good time. Suddenly, something struck me in the face. The blow was so hard that it knocked my glasses into my lap. It really hurt. I turned around to the patient next to me to inquire, but he was utterly lost in his thoughts and unaware of what he had done. I realized he must have had an involuntary movement, and I had merely been in the way. I calmed down, but I also moved my chair a bit farther from him. In future encounters with my patients, I remembered to keep a safe distance from them. I had learned my lesson.

I was touched by the love and devotion of patients' families and caregivers who never gave up on them but continued daily and weekly to visit and assist them.

Entertainment for the Patients

At Whitby, staff members planned many activities for the patients to help the time pass more pleasantly. I often participated in the activities: going to the mall, eating out, gardening, and seeing a show in the village.

One very sunny afternoon, organizers set up chairs and tables on the lawn. The residents sat in lawn chairs and wore their summer hats. Music was playing, and clowns moved among them with balloons.

Someone had brought a dog and circulated among the guests, and guests, in turn, gave the dog a pat and talked to him. Farther away, residents and staff played ringtoss. In another area, some played lawn croquet. A volleyball tournament was also in progress. A volunteer was serving strawberries, ice cream, and cake, and it seemed that people were enjoying themselves immensely. For a while, their burdens had been set aside while they enjoyed the sun and each other's company.

I sat back to watch a while and realized the friendships I had made among them in the two years I had been there. It was hard to let them go, to set those friendships aside, but it was time for me to leave. I had firmly dedicated myself to the Lord to serve him as a chaplain, wherever he beckoned me. I had been called to Toronto.

I said a silent good-bye to a place in which I had witnessed much suffering but also much of God's grace and in which he strengthened me as I supported those in pain.

Working in a Nursing Home

As we toured the nursing home, we encountered several wings that housed residents who required much assistance and care. Nurses, doctors, physiotherapists, and an activity director were among those who met patients' needs. The retired wing was quite modern and efficient and exuded certain elegance. It was also very busy. Nurses hovered around the residents who were confined to their wheelchairs or their beds.

In one wing, there were residents with disabilities and people who responded very little to their caregivers or families. In this place, I saw a tremendous need for visitors. It was a place where chaplains, volunteers, ministers, and family could bring much love.

What were my impressions when I entered that wing? There was a pervasive mix of odors. Urine, medication, and Bengay liniment mixed together and lingered everywhere in that wing. Doors stood open to the rooms on each side of the main corridor by the nurses' station and the common lounge. The patients' rooms were plain and unadorned, without the flowers and decorations that those in the retired wing enjoyed. Here the atmosphere was most like a hospital.

Music played from several radios, all on different stations, creating a cacophony of noise. Televisions blared. Patients called in tremulous voices or screeched in high-pitched demands. Nearby, someone smashed his fist against wood. A resident sat in her chair, yelling and hitting the tray attached to her chair. Nurses came and went. I stopped beside the angry woman, and she began yelling at me. I, appalled at her skeletal appearance, put my hand on her shoulder. She kept on yelling and angrily pointed her finger at me. I waited a while and caressed her shoulder. She calmed down, but did not look at me anymore. I knelt down so she could look into my face, but she was lost in her world. After a while, I stood and said good-bye to her.

I entered the lounge where the television blared. Two or three people sat impassive in their wheelchairs. I stopped by each one, took a hand in mine, and said hello. Some looked into my face; others sat with their head pressed against their chest. For those who looked down, I knelt so they could see my face. I smiled and placed my hand close so they could touch my hand if they chose to.

Continuing on my rounds, I entered another room and stopped just as suddenly. A strange sensation gripped me, and a chill ran down my spine. The room was dark; the curtains were drawn. There were no decorations or flowers. Two skeletal figures were lying in their beds. I paused by each bed, one at a time, took a hand in mine, and said a few words of greeting. No response. I sat near the beds where I could see their faces. Their mouths hung open, and their eyes were focused somewhere else in the room. They seemed totally cut off from other humans … cut off in every social way. They existed; that was about all.

I think this is what Jesus meant when he said, "I was sick, and you visited me." Though there was no response, I stayed a while with these silent patients.

You might ask, "Why do you stay?" I keep in mind that, perhaps hidden inside, some part of these people may be aware of my presence. I stay because I want to give them the gift of my presence. I stay because I care. I don't want to think the grandiose idea that I do it for Christ. Yet, at that moment, I felt a great love for him because he enabled me to be in that place at that moment, where I could give a lot of my care. I felt his presence in that dingy, dark room, and I humbly thanked him for revealing himself to us.

It was humbling to walk through those rooms. Some residents showed their pleasure when I talked with them or touched them gently. What I gave seemed so little that I didn't think it could count, yet it seemed to mean so much to them. I was able to forget about myself when I walked among these people and concentrate only on what

I could do for each of them. Each one taught me a new way to reach them, and I could only humbly accept it.

In this home, my work was low-key and quiet. It was a job of which I could write little. Yet it helped me to learn so much about the world of an elderly person, to grow in understanding, and to know how to respond. It had become a necessary part of my life. I had no other motive than to show these people I cared enough for them to come and see them whenever I was in the building.

The Second Floor

The second floor of the home was immensely different, so different that it seemed they were two separate buildings. It contained apartments, some for couples and others for single patients. They were similar to luxury apartments, but were built for the comfort and care of elderly people and separate from other units on the first floor. They were beautifully decorated and furnished, often with the residents' own furniture and possessions.

On one occasion, I met a lady who moved about in an electric wheelchair and communicated with an alphabet board. When I asked about the woman's circumstances, the nurse told me that her condition was due to a previous illness that had brought on a coma. The nurse thought the woman had aspiration pneumonia, which left her unable to talk.

During our first visit, the woman was quite open and friendly. Through her board, she communicated with me at length, telling me that she had three children and saying she would soon go home to live with one of them. She seemed content, visited with other residents as much as she could, and participated in the programs offered at the home. Other times when I came to see her, she communicated that she was busy and did not want to visit, although she was still quite friendly.

After a while, I wondered if she were giving me the brush-off, and I thought perhaps I had got my signals wrong, or I had, quite unaware, offended her or been overbearing. Perhaps she felt I would talk to her about religion, and she did not want to pursue that subject. I did not press upon her, but felt uncomfortable. I was unsure if I should visit her again. The director of the home told me to let her be. It was sometimes just difficult to understand what she wanted.

However, for the duration of my time at the home, I made an effort to talk to her for a while, when I met her.

Another time, one of the residents, a very distinguished gentleman in his late seventies, offered me an afternoon of pure musical enjoyment. Fred played the organ very well, even playing for the services they had in the chapel. He had recorded tapes of his music, which he shared with the people around him. His children visited him regularly, and he often went out for dinner with them or to other activities in town. He was healthy and enjoyed life. He often talked of his wife, how they had enjoyed travelling and attending concerts together before she died. He played old English and war melodies that brought tears to my eyes, especially my favorite song, "Roses of Picardy." It was good to see that he still "blossomed in his old age and bore fruits" by serenading staff and residents with his music.

Loss of Independence

One thing that disturbed the elderly people most was that they couldn't lock their own door, thus losing privacy and independence. They had to depend on other people for transportation and all the many details of their lives, including self-care they hadn't been able to manage alone. What they also found very distressing was that they couldn't have their family and friends around when they needed or wanted them to be there. For some friends and family members, a visit to the nursing home might be a long trip requiring a lot of planning. Additionally, knowing that a loved one is forced to live such a regimented and restricted life may also trigger unpleasant thoughts and feelings within themselves, emotions they may not be ready to deal with, including feelings of guilt with some ambivalence tied in. While it might be necessary to keep their loved ones in the nursing home, family members and friends may also feel a sense of great loss, of missing the loved one who is no longer living at home.

Another Wing

Retired people, couples or singles who lived in apartments, occupied this part of the nursing home. Some dwelling units were larger than others were, but all of them had access to lounges, kitchens, dining rooms, and craft rooms.

I visited the couples there sometimes. One afternoon, Kay invited me to see the home she shared with her husband, Joe, a spacious apartment with several pieces of furniture from their home that made the place look very elegant and homey. Kay and Joe came to this place from New Brunswick so they could stay together and get some assistance because Joe had Alzheimer's disease. The couple had four children. One lived nearby.

Despite Joe's condition, Kay couldn't put her husband in an institution, but rather she wanted to look after him herself as long as she could. Tearfully, she told me how she worried that something would happen to her, and then Joe would have to move, maybe placed in a mental institution or in another home. She worried that nursing staff might not look after him as well as she did and they might make fun of his idiosyncrasies and let him wander around. She said Joe had once been helpful around the house, but now he couldn't even read the paper or put on a sweater. She had to do almost everything for him.

At night, he wouldn't sleep. He wandered around the apartment, causing Kay sleepless nights. I engaged Joe in conversation. He talked about being safe on the road and that cars could hit him. I sensed Kay's nervousness while he talked, so I smiled reassuringly at her. She quickly explained to me that Joe had been in a car accident. From that time on, he had deteriorated greatly. She said, too, that, while she sometimes talked to him, he would ask her where Kay was.

"After forty-six years together, it's pure agony to realize he doesn't even know I'm here with him."

The intimacy of this couple was gone, and Kay felt alone and frustrated. How long would this go on? She shook her head. "It would have been better if he had died instead of being a stranger in my life. He's so unpredictable. I lock the door at night, but he has learned to open it, so I have to watch constantly that he isn't wandering around or going outside."

I told her that God loved Joe infinitely and knew who he was, even though Joe was like a stranger for us.

"Tell me more about God's love. I need that."

I told her about the God I knew, the Lord I followed faithfully in my life and who never disappointed me—the Lord in whom I hoped for my future. She listened and appeared encouraged. She asked how she could know God in that way.

"I follow God from the moment I get up in the morning until I lay down to sleep at night." I told her what it means to be a child of God.

When it was time for me to leave, she asked me to come again and stay for tea. They loved to have visitors.

When I got home that night, I was grateful that my husband held me in his arms. He told me later how much he loved me. When he did, I thought of Joe and Kay. What an agony for her to live with a spouse who wasn't the one she knew and loved. In circumstances like that, it is like living with a stranger walled within another world.

Blossoming through Many Activities

One morning, I led a discussion group in one of the brightly lit lounges. A soft breeze and the scent of many flowers wafted in through the windows as we sat comfortably together, some of us on couches and others in their wheelchairs. Each one started by saying something about his or her life before coming to the nursing home. Then I asked each of them to consider this question: "How has your life changed since you moved here?"

The purpose of this gathering was to foster communication between the residents. In only a short while, they were talking to each other, asking and answering questions of each other and sympathizing with each other. By learning about someone else's situation, they found out that their own wasn't as bad as they thought and they weren't alone in their feelings.

Then one woman began to cry. She related how different it was for her to see her son and her friends. Her son had his own life and couldn't spend much time visiting her. She had suddenly become dependent on many people to take her out and do things for her after being able to do everything by herself—as well as helping others—that waiting for people to come and assist her made her feel very tied down and isolated. Her fellow patients sympathized, each of them identifying with this woman's needs and her feeling of loss.

One man said, "It's like being a baby again. And those who help us sometimes do so with such patronization, as if I've also lost my intellect. Just sad."

The group went on talking, seemingly with a desire to get closer to one another and to have a relationship with those they met in the hall other than just saying a passing hello. There seemed to be a real empathy and camaraderie among them. As they returned to their rooms, they said it had been good to be together. The results of such a simple activity thrilled me, and I hoped we would have many more opportunities to meet, share, and heal.

Louise

Some of the staff pointed out a resident named Louise who was still in her early sixties, one of the youngest residents at the home. They were very concerned about her because of her suicidal intentions and asked me to spend time with her.

Louise could be very charming and self-giving at times, hugging everybody, smiling constantly, and helping around the home in many ways. Other times, I found her on her bed, weeping, very depressed, and full of self-pity. I came to know her story a little at a time.

She came to the home a year after her husband died, when she was unable to keep her apartment by herself. Her daughter visited occasionally, but not as often and as affectionately as Louise would have liked. Louise had many complaints.

She missed her husband terribly and said her roommates were not friendly, the staff wasn't very caring, and her daughter wasn't good company. Her daughter worked as a volunteer at a center for handicapped people. Louise felt her daughter was good at her work, but there were days when she didn't feel up to taking the bus to go to work.

Louise was grateful for my company and tried to become close to me for a while, but then she plunged into her depression and didn't want to be with me. Then she felt like ending her life, as if it weren't worth living. All she wanted to do was close her eyes and go. In those moods, she became quite unpleasant to herself, me, and those around her.

When that happened, I invited her to go for a walk in the garden. When she came with me, I asked if she wanted to share anything about her life with her husband. She stopped to admire many of the flowers and laughed contentedly, happy to be out there with a friend. She shared some memories of her husband, and we talked about the time she had with her husband. She realized she had many good memories of him. I also asked her about the things she enjoyed that could help when she was having a bad day.

"Look for me any time you feel this depression coming on," I said. "We could go to the garden again and enjoy its beauty." Then we prayed together for comfort, the strength to chase away suicidal thoughts, the ability to keep good memories present, and love for the Lord and her family.

She said she realized that every new day was a gift from God and she should enjoy it while she was still in good health. I suggested she get to know some of the residents and take them for a ride in their wheelchairs, bring them near the windows, or ask permission to take them outside to enjoy the sunshine and the flowers. She could also listen to Fred play the organ.

A new light was in her eyes, and I silently prayed that it would last. I kept company with her during the weeks of my placement at the home, and she appeared to be improving a bit, so much so that even the staff noticed the turnaround. At the same time, her doctor continued monitoring her moods, but, on the whole, she seemed well.

However, I worried that her improvement would only last for a while and, when winter came, she would plunge again into depression because that was the time she struggled most. I also knew that time is a great healer, and I hoped she'd gradually recover from her deep grief and come to enjoy life to its fullest extent. She eventually was situated in a retirement home, where she was closer to her family and her spirit lifted up considerably.

Precious in His Sight

I came to know a lady in her eighties who I only knew as Mrs. Barrett. She gave me so much delight that I visited her as often as I could. She lived in a beautifully decorated apartment within the care facility. She was always well dressed and groomed. She had angina, a sign of underlying heart disease, and was terminally ill with cancer.

Though doctors discovered that her cancer was growing very fast and she might only live a few months more, when I visited her, she appeared calm and rational. She talked about her disease with dignity and awareness and without complaining. She decided not to have an operation because she felt that, with her age and angina condition, it might be risky.

Her wish was to live the rest of her life peacefully at the home where she had made a lot of friends. She had taken care of her personal affairs. Though she had no children, she kept in touch with her extended family. She cried one day because she hadn't heard from some members of her family after she had told them the news. She felt cut off and wondered if they cared or if they were afraid.

When I spent time with her, I felt as though I was in the company of a much younger person because her spirit was so alert and youthful. She was a very gracious woman who was concerned about everyone around her. We talked a lot about the home, what she had been doing, and the news and happenings there.

Mrs. Barrett had a very old Bible that she often read. I pointed out the passage in Isa 43 (NIV), "Since you are precious and honored in my sight ... and because I love you, I will give men in exchange for you."

"This Bible means so much to me," she told me. "It's the source of my strength. I used to go to church and enjoy it. The minister's wife has come to see me, and I really enjoyed her visit. I feel uncomfortable now when I attend because I sense that people are staring at me. When you have cancer, it seems you are marked or something." She laughed with me.

"I walk with my God, and he helps me to go through each day of my life. When the pain will be too much for me to bear, I trust the doctor will give me the right medication to manage the pain. I have come to accept my life in a serene way. I know I can't change anything, and I just take things one day at the time."

One day, we were having a long conversation when she told me that the doctor wanted to take another test to see how the disease was progressing. At first, she resisted. "What's the use of all these tests?" she asked. But then she changed her mind.

"What made you change your mind?"

"There are things happening. I don't know if they are things from the inside or outside. I want to know where they are happening and how they make me feel. I want the doctors to find out as much as they can so they can help someone else with the same condition. I can't think only of myself. Now this thing will be over soon, in a few months, they say, but, for others, it will continue, and the doctors can study all the developments with me."

Admiration for this great woman filled me as I left her room that day. She seemed to have all things in hand and to have made her peace with her disease. She showed great courage and strength.

An Outdoor Party

The nursing home staff planned many events for the residents. One day, they took residents for a walk around the neighborhood both those in wheelchairs and those who could still walk under their own power. It made a long line around the block. I joined them with delight and walked arm in arm with a woman whose steps were not so sure.

We talked amicably during our walk and enjoyed each other's company. Another time, the residents enjoyed lawn bowling or some quiet games in the lower auditorium. There were pet shows with animals groomed for the occasion.

One morning when I arrived, I saw a group of ladies on the patio cleaning strawberries for a party that afternoon. They were all chatting and seemed to be having a good time. Louise was there, directing the job.

"I have done more eating than cleaning," one lady said to me. "I guess I won't be able to eat lunch." We giggled together like two young girls.

Summer had arrived, and I would soon leave and complete my work at the home. I felt sad because I had made a lot of friends and they had all taught me so much. I asked the director if I could stay as a part-time chaplain, but there was no budget for that position. Visiting clergy from the community filled that need.

On my last week there, I arrived at the home on a clear, sunny morning and found a big party going on in the large garden. People in wheelchairs were tending plants in raised flowerbeds while others were strolling around the grounds, and still others sat by the pond. A group of men, including Fred and Joe, were leaning against their shovels and talking. I had no idea what they were supposed to be doing, but they seemed to be having a great time together, laughing cordially.

Mrs. Barrett was dressed in navy and white and wore a large, white hat. She sat in the gazebo, drinking lemonade with other ladies who also wore pretty hats. I spotted Louise serving lemonade. Flowers adorned her straw hat, and she appeared cheerful and confident that day, something I had observed other times when she waited on others. I mentioned this to one of the nurses who agreed with my assessment and said they'd try to keep her busy.

The residents seemed to have an enjoyable time, laughing, talking, and taking advantage of a perfect summer day. Then I noticed someone who appeared very distressed, so I approached her. I joined her by the pond where she sat pulling weeds.

"Enid, are you not enjoying the party?"

"I used to have a big garden, too, with lots of flowers. I want to go home. Can you take me home, please?"

"I'm sorry, Enid. I can't do that. Perhaps your children will come to visit you."

I stayed with her for a while and talked about the flowers, the big hats everyone was wearing, and the food that was being prepared for the barbecue. Pulling weeds seemed to distract her, and I left her to talk to other residents.

Saying Good-bye

It was time for me to go, to leave this party and these people. I paused at the entrance of the garden to watch the camaraderie and listen to the music and laughter. Many of these people had become close to me, and I truly appreciated them. I knew the happy time may have been only for a while, and I felt Enid following me with her eyes. However, I was leaving with a happy image, and I was pleased with the time I had spent there.

A few months later, the director of the home told me that Mrs. Barrett had passed away peacefully. One of her last thoughts was for me, how great and refreshing it had been to have someone to talk with who understood her and did not try to change her mind, but respected her faith in God.

St. Joseph's Hospital

Visitors who enter St. Joseph's Hospital in Brantford, Ontario, will see an open chapel at the end of one corridor. Its quiet atmosphere invites people to meditate and pray. Next to the chapel is the department of pastoral care services. I worked there as a member of the pastoral care team.

People who work in pastoral care are chaplains and companions to patients who suffer from a variety of illnesses. Chaplains focus on the spiritual journey of each individual they visit, while acknowledging their differing backgrounds. They see patients as spiritual beings as well as physical ones, and they deal with patients' relationships to themselves, others, and God.

In my studies, I recognized that unprocessed grief may trigger detrimental changes in the human body and people can become ill after the death of a relative or loss of something precious. Even a change in people's lifestyle may precipitate a change in their bodies. Reactive illness is a concern for the chaplain who looks into the whole life and environment of the patients so they can "companion" them through their illness.

One of the most important tasks of pastoral care is to listen to the patient, family members, and the medical staff. The chaplain listens actively for clues indicating hidden feelings behind the words he or she hears, information and emotion the patient may feel no one else cares about. The chaplain does not have to say much, but acknowledges what is confided. Often after a lengthy monologue, a patient will exclaim, "Oh, I feel so much better now that I have it let it all out."

Allowing patients to talk about their worries and fears can be a great release for them, but there are times that a chaplain can offer only the ministry of presence, as in being at the side of the person who may be unresponsive, in a coma or in a palliative state. A chaplain can hold a hand or look into the eyes of the patient with warmth and care. Words are not always necessary or helpful. The touch and vibrations of concern transmit their messages even to unresponsive people. Steady, faithful visits also convey the message that the chaplain is one who cares. As I reflected on these aspects of my work, I realized that working at St. Joseph's gave me many opportunities to practice that presence.

Keeping Watch

One night, I had been called to stay with a patient who was transferred to another hospital. As I had nothing to do, but just sit and watch, I decided to write down a few reflections on this particular case. Later on, in the week, I reviewed them and put them in order. Then I showed them to my supervisor and we talked a bit about them. She found them very revealing about a lonely time. Here I transpose those thoughts in this chapter:

It is late in the afternoon. I have finished my calls set out for the day. Yet something compels me to sit by the bed of this very sick woman and just be there. I remain silent and still. In these moments, I feel Jesus inviting me to go to the garden with him. He invites me to help him in his agony through the suffering of this woman, as if he were whispering, "Could you watch and stay with her for a while? You are with me."

It should be easy to sit more comfortably in my chair and be present in the dim room, but I question what I'm doing. Why do I stay at the end of my workday when I'm no longer productive? I'm not saying anything edifying to this woman. I'm not even touching her because she has withdrawn from my touch. The air in this room is warm and stale. I don't like its smell and would like to be somewhere else.

In the garden, Jesus needed the alert presence of his friends, to be there with him as he faced a time of suffering. He asked them to watch with him. The gospel of Luke tells us that his sweat was like drops of blood falling to the ground. He needed the alert presence of someone who cared enough to be there, watching with him.

The disciples failed him because they questioned their productivity, their purpose for being there in the dark garden. They wanted to go to sleep. They did not realize the depth of pain and anguish their master and friend suffered that night. They could not think beyond their own need for sleep and comfort.

Here I am in the same situation, facing a person in great pain and questioning myself because I'm not doing anything. I don't see myself keeping watch over a person who is alone, scared, and feeling no hope. I even question God's intervention. Where was God in Jesus' most difficult hours? How could he leave him alone in the hands of angry mobs?

I can't answer those questions just as I can't answer my questions why God is not doing something for this woman in pain. Ambulance workers will soon move her to another hospital because the staff at this hospital can't do anything more for her.

Is there anyone on earth or in heaven who can do something for her? I humbly acknowledge that I do not know who can give me an answer and I'm simply an instrument of service in this universe. Questions too big for me remain unanswered. Once more, I have to admit that now I know in part, but there will come a time when I will see the Lord face to face and learn all the answers from him.

I suddenly realize that, after his time in the garden, Jesus faced the horror of his death. I don't have to face death, but I have a pleasant evening at home ahead of me. My selfishness stuns me. I question my productivity not for the sake of the patient, but for the sake of going home with a clear conscience of a job well done. I'm accountable in my work, according to the need that stares at me. I want to go home with a clear conscience that I have accomplished something good that day.

Again, I look at the suffering patient. Her breathing is labored; her color is gray. She does not look well. Maybe she will not survive until the ambulance workers come for her. What else can I do? Tears fill my eyes as I realize how much I would like to do for her, but I'm so limited. Then I hear a tender voice whisper to me, "Stay with her and keep watch with me."

I do not know if the sick woman feels my presence and if she realizes she is not alone. Do vibrations flow from me to embrace her in some way, reassuring her of my comfort and concern? If so, it may give her some strength to fight and go on. All is not lost if there is someone to encourage and support her.

Humbly, I acknowledge my task is now to watch and be present to this person whose life is slipping away. And I thank the Lord to have led me through this dark hour to the realization that, in the end, I am productive according to his plans.

I Was a Stranger

In the past few months in a new town, I have learned that it is a friendly place. I was a complete stranger, but the circle of people I came to know kept widening every week. They made me feel welcome and part of the town.

At the beginning of my stay here, I found it hard when I had to wait for the bus and transfers. I was used to driving my car, which my husband now used. However, as the days went by, my eyes opened to enjoyable aspects of a new place. It happened as I traveled to and from work in a strange town. They were things I might not have otherwise noticed or felt. They became gifts dropped into my life to make it more pleasant.

When it snowed, the world greeted me in stillness as I walked out the door in the morning. A soft, white, and unmarred blanket covered everything. A kind of magic hung in the air. It looked as I stepped into fairyland.

As I walked to the bus stop, elderly people on their morning stroll greeted me cheerfully, even though they did not know me. My steps became brisker then because they made me feel noticed and worthwhile. I reached the bus stop. A teacher who also waited for the bus to go to school greeted me cheerfully. She recounted some of her adventures in the classroom in such a pleasant and easy attitude that she held my attention. I did not feel the cold then, and the bus came in time.

At the depot downtown, a group of disabled people was waiting for a special bus to take them to work. It was a pleasure to watch them. They were always cheerful and good to each other. They exchanged greetings, hugs and handshakes, cigarettes, candies, and news. They joked and poked each other. They were glad to see their friends and so warm in their encounters that one forgot their disabilities.

Every day, they showed the world a lesson in acceptance and goodwill toward each other. They often greeted me, a total stranger, and smiled in such a fine and simple way that one's heart overflowed with gladness. As I settled on my bus, I couldn't help but feel that I was glad to belong to the human race.

Attitudes of Patients and Families

The first signs of spring became visible all around us. We just had to be alert enough to catch them. Most people I met appeared to be waiting for spring with exultant hearts, yet, for those in hospital who appear so lifeless and dejected, I wished I could bring them some of those grand hopes and expectations. Some patients would say wistfully, "Perhaps I will be better in spring." Every day, I worked on my skills to help them. My hope was not to become so complacent that I did not work any longer to better myself. I still had much to learn as a chaplain.

Some people started to connect with me, and I think it may have been that they appreciated my friendly approach and my interest in their well-being, while others would show only a cold, distant response to my approach. They did not want my interference. Still others asked for prayer and to hold my hand as a sign they wanted guidance and direction while they poured their hearts out. They touched me deeply.

With all of them, I became aware of whom I represented. That thought kept me in awe of the great responsibility I carried. I found out so many little things I could do for the patients. My care was becoming more about quality than quantity. I strove to go deeper into their personality to understand their pain and the story behind it.

When I asked a patient how he considered his illness, he said that he has served the Lord for many years. He was faithful in his church and involved in many activities there. Although he now was concerned for his difficulties, I sensed he had peace within himself.

Many of these patients became my friends, and I loved them dearly. Then I tried to do little things to bring them comfort, such as reading their favorite book or the Bible, giving them some fresh water, adjusting the bed or their covers on their bed so they were more comfortable, opening a curtain, and so on. I wished I could do more for them. I blessed the moment I was at my home with my family, but I remembered those people I left behind, who had to stay there.

On the fourth floor at St. Joseph's, I encountered people with unusual and complex illnesses. At times, they were frustrated over their long stay in the hospital where they did not seem to improve. Other patients were frightened of their pain or of the treatment ahead. When I sat by them and listened, they let their burdens out and then felt less frightened.

There were families who made many sacrifices to help their loved ones. At times, family members became very demanding of the staff, or they did not understand the care and methods of treatment given to their loved one. They often passed the whole night with their family member and then took a break in the lounge. The staff and I worked together to offer comfort, understanding, and empathy to these people in agony for their loved one. Chaplains and staff also offered explanations about conditions and treatment when patients or their family members asked questions.

As I walked along the corridors, I stopped at the nurses' station. In the dining room across from the station, a number of patients sat in wheelchairs. Some patients were asleep while others looked vacantly into space or babbled to themselves.

A sense of deep compassion overcame me, as I walked to them. I put my arms around a lady's shoulders, and she babbled something to me. I did not understand, but I smiled at her and caressed her head. Another gentleman had let his blanket slip to the floor. He was uncovered from the waist down, but quite unaware of his exposure. I covered him and spoke reassuringly to him.

In their younger years, these patients would have been appalled and saddened if they knew how much they would change, but, at this time, those same people have become completely dependent on others. They make no sense when they talk and seem to have lost their dignity and sense of propriety. Yet they are still children of God, and God loves them as the children he has created.

I thought that the cycle of life goes on inexorably and changes us, sometimes for the worse, as in the case of dementia and Alzheimer's disease. It is difficult to remember that these people are still God's creatures when they act out of their illness and not like the persons they used to be. Even when we lose patience with them because we cannot understand their behavior, they are entitled to our love, respect, and veneration for all they have given in life. And as difficult as it may seem, one day, some of us may be like them.

Praying with a Buddhist Family

St. Joseph's has always strived to be open to people of every walk of life, faith, and culture. Its motto ("It is an honor to serve the sick") is what the staff practice daily. Therefore, we had people from all corners of the world with many varying beliefs and lifestyles, and we did our best to meet their needs.

As a chaplain, I was a friend, a shoulder to cry on, a strong arm to lean on, a companion through trying times, a listener for people with troubled and complicated lives, a reminder of God's forgiveness, and, on some occasions, an interpreter for Spanish and Italian people who spoke little English.

At St. Joseph's, I immersed myself in learning, in understanding the pastoral visit as the development of a relationship through the gentle unfolding of the patient's story. The chaplain should not program the visit, but let it develop naturally and comfortably, following the patient's direction. I learned that patients would relate their own experiences and burden in their own time at their own pace and the chaplain should be alert to the verbal and nonverbal messages a patient may give. Sometimes, what is not expressed in words can be transmitted in body language.

On my floor, I met an East Indian woman whose family came to visit her every day. I first noticed that they were usually quiet around her, almost reverent. They all looked handsome and strikingly beautiful. The men were not very tall, but had well-groomed dark hair and perfect teeth. They were well mannered and polite.

The ladies and children were attractive, too, with wavy hair and smiling faces. The women dressed in our Western style rather than saris. The children, who spent a lot of time looking at the fish tank we had in the hall, were always well behaved. One daughter spent her time with her sick mother, reading their holy book that someone had carefully wrapped in a piece of silk. She told me that she prayed her mother would not suffer long.

Even the sick lady had a beauty of her own, faded a bit from age and illness. Many picture of their gods and symbols of their faith surrounded her, a contrast to the Advent season and the gold and silver decorations that glittered everywhere in the unit and strings of lights that lit the hall while Christmas songs played softly on the radio.

I sat in the hall by one young woman with her children and talked with her about her mother-in-law's condition. She said her family did not think their mother would make it, but they prayed she would not suffer. I asked her about her belief in prayer. We found points of contact between our faiths. I also asked her how they felt with the Christmas decorations all around.

She smiled. "We make feast at Christmas. We do not celebrate like you do with church services and music, but we have a big family dinner, and we exchange gifts. We do it especially for the children, and it is a good feast of family togetherness. This year, our mother will not be with us, and we will not do much, just something for the children. We appreciate the culture we found in this country, and we follow what we can with all of you Canadians."

We talked for a while. I asked the children if they enjoyed their school and snow games, and then I asked the young woman if I could do something for them as a family.

She asked, "Can you pray for her? Your God is just as good as ours is. We know he loves everyone."

We went back to the room of the sick mother, and I told the other family members what I was going to do. They agreed respectfully, and I prayed with them in an inclusive form, for their loved one, for them, and for their children in this time of need. The ladies hugged me; their eyes glistened with tears. I stayed with the family for a while and got to know them a little better. I learned about their life and work. I felt this experience greatly enriched me.

Searching for Forgiveness

There are times when even the intervention of a chaplain, a representative of God, fails to bring about the results we hope for. It appears that the individual we seek to counsel is lost in his or her convictions of sin and hopelessness and all our efforts and prayers do not bring peace and change in that person. It happens from time to time, and the key is not to lose courage but to persevere in our ministry of faith. Such a case came to my attention one evening.

Bill, a man on the third floor, had problems with his legs. The call came in one night when I was on duty, and I needed to go and visit him right away because both the man and his wife were greatly distressed. When I met Bill, he was sitting in his wheelchair in the dining room. I saw a look of utter desperation in his body posture and eyes. He told me that, during the war, he was a gunner and had to kill as many enemies as possible. He had killed many. Now great remorse faced him. Because his life was passing by, he was desperate to be forgiven for such a crime.

"Bill, you have to think that you may shoot at many people during the war, but really kill just a few because you probably missed many. It was an order you had to obey. In war, that's the law. If you are in it, you have to defend your country and yourself and keep going."

As I said this, I realized how weak and futile my words must have been against his pain, but I stayed with him and his wife.

"Oh, no," he said. "When I shot them, I made sure they died. It was my intention to kill the enemy. I hated them. And now, what will my future be when I die? Will I be forgiven?"

So much despair was in his voice that his wife put her arms around him and consoled him. "Do not be upset so much, my dear. We will resolve this, too. Now you just have to get better."

I tried again with different words, "Bill, in the Bible, God says he sent his son Jesus to the cross as a sacrifice for us so we can be washed from our sins, whatever they are. We are made acceptable in God's sight so we can have eternal life with him. He can forgive you because he loves you. Do you believe and accept this?"

"Oh, I'm not sure what to believe anymore. Maybe God can forgive me. I do not know." He wiped tears from his eyes.

"Try to think about it," I said gently. "Repeat the words simply, and be still. I forgive you. We all forgive you. You have to start by forgiving yourself, and then God will give you the peace that you seek."

After a while, I left. The next day, I related Bill's story to Kathy, the chaplain on his floor. She promised to follow up with him. When he left the hospital after a while, he was much better, yet Kathy said he was still asking to be forgiven.

Sometimes, our words are well intentioned, and we place so much power in them, but they may fail to penetrate a heart that has endured a lot in life and become hardened. We know there is forgiveness for everybody, but not everyone accepts it. That is the dilemma.

Renewed Memories

Therapists kept the patients occupied with various exercises and activities. Some patients participated with enthusiasm while others sat still and apathetic throughout the session. However, they all strived to exercise and walk a bit. Walking seemed to be the favorite activity of many because being able to do so made them proud and independent. The patients who were bedridden, unresponsive, and uncommunicative were quite another matter. The therapists, nurses, their families, and I tried to stimulate them in every possible way. Their families brought pictures, plants, and favorite objects from home, and people sometimes brought in pets to cheer them.

Through the years, I gathered illustrated books, and I used them with patients who were unable to participate in other activities. Ted, a dementia patient who stayed in bed most of the time, closed up within himself and barely responded to anyone. I brought one of my favorite gardening books for him to see. With his daughter at his side, we looked through the pages and commented on and appreciated the pictures of flowers and gardens.

When we reached a certain page showing a garden with many varieties of flowers, Ted whispered, "Flowers … flowers … my garden … so nice."

I looked at his daughter. She smiled. She was glad to hear him talk. She explained that Ted had been an avid gardener and had a beautiful garden all his life with many of those same flowers that were shown on the page. His daughter and I agreed that pictures could restore memories and bring them to the surface, even when other things were forgotten. I left the book with Ted for a while and continued with other books and other patients. Sometimes, these efforts with unresponsive patients meet with success.

What Shall We Do with Our Pets?

Another of our monthly activities for the patients was the pet show. On that day, family members and friends of residents brought their cats, dogs, or birds to visit. The pets were usually well behaved and well groomed. The patients enjoyed seeing the animals and petting them.

At home, we had a dog, Schatzie, who was completely black with long, wavy hair. She was part Labrador and part German shepherd. We were proud of Schatzie because she was very wise and intelligent for an animal of her kind. My daughter, Giselle, and I decided to bring her to the hospital for the pet show and see what happened. Giselle groomed Schatzie so she would look her best, and Schatzie behaved so well you would have thought she did that every day. She walked and stopped by each patient while Giselle talked to her. She waited while patients admired and petted her. I was so proud of both my dog and my daughter for their part, and I noticed the patients were cheered a bit during the show. They talked to each other and smiled.

At one show, we had a white parakeet. With small skates on his feet, he skated back and forth across the table. He whistled as he skated, to the delight and laughter of everyone, and he seemed to enjoy entertaining as much as people enjoyed watching him. Afterward, his owner made the rounds with him to see each patient, who petted, admired, and praised him. Oh, he loved every minute of it. Then he suddenly settled on a woman's lap and did not move anymore. Imagine the reaction of this lady. She was so proud that she stayed sitting and kept petting the bird and smiling happily.

It may seem a little thing to bring pets for such a show and for the animals to be admired and petted, but the joy and the pleasant smiles of our patients rewarded us. Those little creatures bring much affection and comfort to the life of a human being, especially when entertainment and mobility are so limited.

Hymn Singing

When I arrived at St. Joseph's, I noticed there was no piano on any floor, so I asked my supervisor if we could get one. Kathy, the other chaplain, worked with administration, and they were able to buy a beautiful piano. I intended to have hymn singing in the dining rooms for staff and patients. We advertised the hymn sing around the hospital, and, little by little, it happened. With the help of hospital staff, we found several volunteer pianists. We sang old songs and old hymns that brought tears to many eyes as they remembered their pleasurable times in their youth.

One time, a staff member brought a patient in a geriatric chair. This woman had never talked to us, and we were surprised to see her participate. When we sang "Blessed Assurance," she joined us with gusto and did not need a hymnbook. She knew all the words by heart. We were thrilled to realize what music had done for her spirit, reminding her of words she had learned in the past and of singing in her church.

Because the activity proved so beneficial to the patients, we continued it for many years with the enthusiastic help of volunteers. Responses from patients ranged from a few tears to smiles and clapping of hands. The music brought a powerful healing force into the patients' lives and, along with it, a sense of well-being and hope for better things to come.

A Country Kitchen

There were days when I arrived on the fourth floor of St. Joseph's to a wonderful aroma. It came from Jessie's Country Kitchen, a venture created by the manager of recreation therapy to create a home-like atmosphere there in the hospital. Jessie was always baking something in her kitchen and involving patients in the activity.

Many mornings, I found a group gathered around Jessie's table, peeling apples for pies or baking cookies or something else as mouthwatering. Jessie and her helpers chatted in a friendly way as they worked, creating a homey atmosphere. They were using whatever ability they had while they worked together. Men and women gathered there and recounted tales of childhood— in their grandmother's kitchen or in their own kitchen—of favorite dishes and developing recipes. It took their mind away from the difficulty of hospital life, medications, and treatments.

Jessie would often offer them tea and toast, and, in that simple act, they felt well cared for. A part of that room was set aside for doing crafts and contained many craft materials. Around Christmastime, there was the fresh scent of eucalyptus and spruce, which patients and therapists used to create Christmas wreaths and decorations that they sold at the semi-annual bazaars. Handmade ornaments decorated the halls of the hospital, and it truly helped them to feel at home.

Raffles were another source of income for the hospital. One year, I won a white and gold ceramic Christmas tree with tiny ornaments on its boughs. An electric light bulb inside lit the ornaments when the tree was plugged into an outlet. One of the patients, who had owned a clay studio before coming to the hospital, crafted the tree. She had given lessons to other patients how to make lovely objects of clay and paint them.

I sat with patients during craft time or baking lessons because I enjoyed seeing their hands at work, using skills they hadn't forgotten but that had gone unused in a while. I delighted to hear them reminisce, a time that sometimes brought tears or, other times, shrieks of laughter.

The patients taught us to hold precious what life we have and to enjoy life at its utmost, no matter what disease we may have. Life is precious. It is God's gift to everyone. It was hard to explain this concept to some family members and patients who wanted their life to be over.

They would say, "Even an animal is better treated because we put it down when it suffers so much. Why not my mother, who is suffering so cruelly and does not want to go on?"

It was a tremendously difficult and ethical argument that staff members did their best to answer. The nurses and the doctors agree to the Hippocratic Oath (to preserve life). We as Christian caregivers know we are not to end the life God gave us, but to use it the best way we can, as difficult as it may be at times.

So, in Jessie's Country Kitchen, we found the warmth and memories of home, a place patients had left behind for a time. There was fellowship, good things to eat, and pretty and useful things to make. For a few hours in a day, life felt closer to normal for patients who gathered there.

Chapter 4

Through the Valley of Death

Mammy

The thought of how lonely the dead must "feel" is unpleasant. It sounds bizarre, considering that people who have died do not feel anything anymore. Or do they?

At each of my parents' funerals, I felt the impulse to stay by the coffin. For some unexplainable reason, I felt they shouldn't be left alone in the cold wind. We had gathered for a funeral service for my mother, whom we called Mammy. Although my siblings and I had essentially accepted the fact that she was gone, we still hurt deeply. She had been such a friend, supporting us and firmly believing in each of her children's potential. It was unthinkable to let her go.

The service was touching. My niece Lizzie sang a hymn that Mammy would have liked. I'm sure she enjoyed it from wherever she was. We went to the cemetery for a brief ceremony by the graveside, and I still felt close to my mother. At its conclusion, when we were leaving, the loss hit me. She was going to stay in that casket all alone, and it was cold. No one would be sitting with her as we had during her illness. This feeling stunned me, but I silently kept walking beside my husband Ernest and my sister Dani, not saying anything. I just kept looking back at that lonely coffin.

That day, I managed to be myself and enjoy our family togetherness. It turned out to be a typical day in North Carolina, warm and dry, and we could sit outside in the garden and visit. From time to time, the memory of that lonely coffin at the cemetery came back to me. What were we doing, leaving Mammy alone? Yet, we couldn't do anything but continue with our lives in the best way we could and keep our mother in our dearest, most precious memories.

Death is such a total and brutal separation from a loved one that it is no wonder so many people go into depression, suicide, or alcoholism, unable to go on with normal life. Even people who know the comfort of Christ have moments of instability at the loss of a loved one. Time is the only healer. Again and again, I have learned that truth, not only in my life, but also in observing the lives and reactions of families and friends who lose someone.

Family Reactions

The reaction of family members at the unexpected death of a loved one may be quite violent and angry at times. One day, I was called to BGH to help a family deal with a sudden death of a patient in his early fifties. In the morning, he had talked to his wife on the phone, eaten breakfast, and sat on his bed a while afterward while chatting with his roommate. He had been doing so well that there was a possibility that he would go home the next week. But by noon, his condition had deteriorated so much that a Code Blue, the code for cardiac arrest, was called.

I hurried to the room with the trained team. They warned me that it might be a difficult case to handle because the family was unprepared. I prayed fervently for the family and for myself to be able to assist them in some way.

The man's wife arrived with two of their children. She screamed in horror at the sight of her husband while the doctor and nurses tried to explain what had happened. She could not and would not listen to anybody. She flung herself on her husband and punched him in the chest.

She screamed, "Why did you do this to me? I'm going to kill you!" She continued in that manner for a while. Her grown children were crying and refusing to be comforted or assisted in any way. For a while, chaos reigned.

With so many people in this small room, all of them under stress, it wasn't long before the air became hot and filled with the odor of perspiration. The vibrations of pain and anger felt like the edge of a knife. His wife cried and said, "I just talked to him this morning. He felt fine. What happened?"

I let them cry and express their feelings. At that moment, there was nothing anybody could do or say to comfort, calm, or support them. They accepted water and Kleenex only, and then they would look at the man in bed and start their outbursts again. After what seemed like hours, they began to calm down. The mother voiced her concern for her youngest son who had been called from high school to come to the hospital.

"I wonder if they told him. I wish I were there with him. He's going to die with this." She cried and then dried her eyes and tried to compose herself.

Thus, we braced for the arrival of the youngest son. The nurses tidied the room, brought in more chairs, moved the second bed outside of the room, and tried to make everyone more comfortable. I offered some words of comfort, wrapped my arms around them, talked to them gently, and prayed with them.

Then the young son arrived. He was angry and full of heated questions. "What is this? Why did it happen? Why did you let him die?" He looked at his father and dropped to the floor, as if in a trance. His sister tried to lift him up, but he started yelling, pushing her away, and pounding his fists on the bed. "Why did you let him die?" He continued to cry for a while and then started wailing, a sound that shocked and scared everyone.

"No, no, don't do that, dear." His mother put her arms around him and rocked him. "It's all right. It's okay," she said, rocking him.

This went on for several hours. When the son finally calmed down, we ushered them to the quiet room, where all of them, exhausted, sat on the couch. The doctor and a nurse soon arrived. In a gentle and sensitive way, they explained, as simply as possible, what had happened. The family listened and asked questions. I sensed that, in some way, they were trying to reason with this event. The young son and his older sister, very pale, sat silent and dejected and stared at the floor. Tears flowed uncontrollably down their faces.

When the doctor and nurse left, I talked to the family and offered words of encouragement, care, and compassion. "In this case, we can only trust that God will look after your loved one, and he is in God's hands always. I understand your pain. He left without suffering because his death was so sudden. I believe he is in a better place where there is no sickness and suffering. I am sorry for you, your children, and your loss. Every time a person leaves, it is like a part of our lives that has gone. God can give us the courage to go on, even during loss."

"Can you pray for us?" one of the children asked.

At their request, we prayed for their dad, the loss of a husband, their lives, and their future without him. I stayed with them until they felt they could leave. As they left, I identified with some of their feelings. They, too, were going to leave their father and husband alone. He would not be going home with them as they had hoped. I prayed that each one of them would find something that might give him or her the strength and the hope he or she needed. I had sensed a very small faith in them, like a weak spark rising up from the embers of a fire.

After many hours of intense grief and an eruption of my own grief, I was exhausted. I sat in my office for a while and reexamined the events of the morning. I offered them to the Lord.

A Courageous Lady

It is amazing how much we can learn from each other and often from the people we least expect. My neighbor of many years, a pleasant woman of southern European descent, came to BGH in a lot of pain. She was diagnosed with cancer, which was spreading rapidly to her lungs. I visited her several times and found out that, in addition to being a gracious friend at home, she was also a courageous person who was determined to get better, go back to her family, and enjoy watching her grandchildren grow. She had a simple, genuine faith, and I often found her reading a religious pamphlet and praying.

Over the years, I had become quite fond of this woman and her husband for their openness, integrity, and friendship. Her ability to converse in English was limited, but she was always most caring and attentive of us.

She later came to the cancer clinic for her treatment. Her husband was always there with her. I visited with them some mornings and thought she looked small and tired while sitting in the big chair with the IV lines attached to her.

We talked mostly about the grandchildren and life in general. She and her husband were most grateful for the clinic that the hospital had opened because they no longer had to endure the drive to Hamilton and spend long hours waiting there for treatment. After months of courageously fighting her illness, my neighbor died. Strangely, I felt empty at the news of her death, along with relief at the thought that her great suffering had ended.

In humility, I acknowledged the gift of courage she gave all of us during her suffering. I thought of all the sickness and discomfort she went through and her determination to overcome it. The cruelty of our life cycles often shatters me. Despite our best efforts to adopt a clean, healthy lifestyle, sooner or later, our bodies develop sickness that we cannot avoid.

After my neighbor's death, I continued to visit the people in the clinic. I learned all of the patients were grateful to the hospital for opening that clinic, saving them great difficulty and much travel. The nurses were very competent and always ready to help. As a visitor, I felt the warm and caring atmosphere.

The thought that illness may touch my family members or me entered my mind. Cancer has touched some of my family members and me. I have survived when others haven't. Every time this dreadful disease strikes someone I know, the thought of my own mortality comes to mind. Humbly, I admit that, like my neighbor, I may also have to face that ordeal. Should that happen, will I have the same courage and the faith my neighbor had?

Thankful for Every Minute of Life

Although I see and attend many deaths, some patients' deaths fill me with sorrow more than others. Part of me has become intertwined with part of those people. They have become friends who walk with me through life for a while.

At the death of one such patient, a longtime resident at St. Joseph's in Brantford, sadness filled me. While the woman was a patient there, I developed a great fondness for her, so her passing made me want to curl up in a chair somewhere and stay there for a while. She had a great sense of humor and could always make everyone laugh. She was very appreciative of the way I dressed. She thought my clothes were beautiful. She joked with me that she would like me to leave my clothes to her when I died because she liked them so much. Every day, she would remind me to be careful with the clothes I was wearing because they would be going to her.

Each month, there was so much death and suffering at that hospital, especially in the palliative care unit. Members of the staff created and organized this special unit to fill a need for dying patients. The unit functions very well with the team providing excellent care to the patient. I usually do not let death touch me too deeply. I go on in my tasks the best I can. I fill my days with work, family, and other activities that I enjoy, keeping feelings of despair and sadness at bay.

I stop to reflect on humankind's mortality, especially on the death of someone whom I know well and care about. Through my work as chaplain, I learned that one goes on living day by day with pain in the best way one can and to be thankful for every minute that comes, more pleasant and pain-free. I believe that's the way to cope.

A Tree that Never Dies

On the grounds of BGH is a tree that has been battered about quite a lot due to building development around the hospital. However, the tree always sprouts new leaves in the spring and continues to grow each year. Now, it stands straight and tall in the garden plot and points to the sky. Like that tree, some patients endure much trauma in their illnesses.

Kim had to undergo several surgeries, each of which left her feeling very depressed and discouraged. The doctor had faith that she could recover, and he was very compassionate and caring in his work. He asked her to look at the tree outside her window and told her how the tree had survived despite all the construction going on around it and how it had managed to live and sprout new leaves every year. He felt her struggle was like the tree and declared that, if it could survive, so could she.

Together with her family and friends, we rallied around her to bring her out of those dark moods. Her friends brought her books, fruit, flowers, and toiletries. I visited her every day, and we talked about clothes, her home, and some of the new books she was reading. Gradually, she became less depressed and upset. She talked more and became interested in things other than her health. She even managed to laugh with us. Then she would go and try a new treatment and afterward talked about the comparison her doctor had made with that tree that stood just outside her window.

Eventually, all the treatments and care failed to improve her health, and it seemed that she would not make it after all. One evening, she told me of her frustration.

"It isn't fair because I'm still young. But I just want to be left alone and die. I've had enough in my life. You always tell me about how much God loves me, but I do not see that. My life has not been the same since my parents died while I was still young. I was left alone to fight such a dreadful and unforgiving disease. Now I only want to die."

I had to respect and accept her words, despite my sadness at hearing them. I did not want to push her. Instead, I prayed with her and hugged her. I told her how good her hair smelled. I also told her I always felt a bit like an elder sister toward her and I would continue to hope and pray for her that she could cope with whatever the future might bring her.

"You're persistent because your faith is strong," she said. "Mine isn't strong anymore after all these years."

She died a few days later. Her friends said it was a relief for her. Something finally went right. I thought how sad it was that she had not made her peace with God. At least she hadn't the last time she talked to me. I hope that, when death approached, she put her hand confidently in the Lord's.

That tree at BGH is still growing and flourishing, reminding me that her spirit is not dead. It is alive in my memory of her.

Sister's Talk

It's so refreshing to have a sister I can chat with. My sister Dani lives far away in North Carolina, but she is as close to me as if she lived on the next street. I love to talk with her about many things, and we seem to understand each other well.

A few weeks ago, we talked about our mother and remembered the things she did or said. Dani took good care of her in her last years, and I will always be grateful to her for that care, for the fact that Mammy had a lovely, comfortable apartment in Dani's house and lived happily with them while watching her grandsons grow.

As we talked of the events that took place before Mammy's death, we considered death itself and shared how we felt. Dani said she sometimes thinks about death, but wasn't afraid of it.

"I just wonder what happens at the moment when the heart stops beating and all organs stop functioning. How do we feel in that instant? Pain, joy, or fear? Of course, no one has ever been able to reopen his or her eyes and tell us what it was like," she mused.

I replied from my experience as a chaplain. "Well, from my work, I can tell you what happened when some patients died. The face seems to cave in, skin color becomes almost greenish, and the person can't respond to us anymore. Then there's the last breath. It's sometimes soundless; it rattles sometimes. Then all is still. Patients might be smiling, or their eyes and mouth are open, and the expression is very somber. Eventually, there is no color in the face and skin. All is finished, all is still, and all is at rest. You feel a great reverence for what has just happened, but then the sadness and pain fills the hearts of those witnessing death. Because I have observed so many deaths and comforted so many mourners, I'm not afraid of it. I just wonder, too, how ready do you really feel at the moment when it comes over your own self and all is finished?"

I feel a lot of pain now when I think of my death, imagining the reaction of my family and loved ones at that happening. I know my children, especially my son, will grieve deeply. I can't help but wonder, "Will they be able to manage without me?" Then I dismiss this thought as nonsense. Of course they will manage. They are grown up and will go on with their lives as best they can.

The idea here is not that death embellishes the person lying in the coffin, but that people wish to prepare the deceased for death because they have compassion and a reverence for life. There are beautiful flower arrangements, soft music, photos, and mementos, so many details to give beauty and reverence to the loved one who has died.

Beauty Also in Death

May was an elderly lady, bedridden most of the time, in St. Joseph's care unit of Brantford. I visited her almost daily and tried to cheer her. She loved to hear me reading to her from her large leather-bound Bible that she kept near her bed. She always wanted to end our reading with her favorite verse, Ps 61:2: "From the ends of the earth I call you, I call as my heart grows faint: lead me to the rock that is higher than I."

With a smile on her lips, she would be lost in her memories when we read those words. She had told me that she and her husband used to sing duets in their church. She and I often quietly sang some of her favorite hymns.

One day, she told me how much she appreciated my visits. "You're such a good, well-trained person for us here in the hospital. Too bad you're not a real minister. But never forget that I love you very much."

Inwardly, I laughed because, although May knew I was a chaplain in the hospital and about my responsibilities there, she had never been able to understand that, even being a woman, I was an ordained Baptist minister.

When she died, I went to the visitation at the funeral home. The room was full of people visiting with her family and each other. There were many flower arrangements, beautiful pictures, and elegant furniture. I looked at her in her coffin, and I was astounded at how young and lovely she looked. She lay there looking very peaceful with a hint of a smile on her lips and her hands lying across her Bible.

Most of the time, she had looked miserable, her hair in disarray, and her hands clutching at the blankets, but death had brought calm and beauty to her person, and I appreciated that transformation.

Where Is My Home?

The weather was gloomy and cold, a true November morning. I stood by the bed of a very sick patient in the palliative care unit at St. Joseph's in Brantford. Tom's condition was unstable, and he was becoming confused and restless. That night, the nurses had found him on the floor of his room with his shoes in his hands. Tom had mumbled that he was trying to go home, to his beloved home.

He often talked to me of how much he missed his home and how he wanted to go there for a while to sit in his favorite chair, read the paper, and see his dog. He missed his loyal companion. He also talked about his cottage at Turkey Point, next to Lake Erie, along with his boat that he used to row across the lake. He also said how much he enjoyed his time there.

At times, he was aware of his condition where he knew he wasn't getting better, but still he wanted to go home, even if only for a little while.

One of the nurses came in with his medication. She gave it to him and talked gently, "How are you this morning, Tom?"

"Oh, the same, I guess," Tom answered vaguely.

"You gave us a bit of scare last night when we found you on the floor in the middle of the room." She leaned toward him, took his hand, and looked at him with great compassion. "I know how badly you want to go home. Perhaps not right now. It's very hard for you to be here, isn't it?" she continued softly.

Tom had tears in his eyes as he nodded. Then he turned to me and said clearly, "I guess I have to get ready for another home. I think I'm ready for that home."

Very gently, I told him, "Yes, your Lord Jesus is ready to welcome you with open arms."

I had come to appreciate this gentleman for his quiet attitude and acceptance of life. Together, we read the paper, and we sometimes discussed some of the issues there. He had been a church warden for many years, and he had loved his work and his church.

When I walked away from my visit with Tom that morning, his nurse's gracious compassion and understanding impressed me. She was busy with many patients on that unit, but she took the time to talk to Tom, understand him, and show that she cared for him.

A few days later, she came to me with tears in her eyes and said that Tom had gone home for good. He was at peace now in his new home in heaven. I thanked her for the grace and care she had shown him, which I had witnessed several times. She had shown me another side of a nurse's busy life. Besides the professional competency and skill that was required for her job, she had also shown caring and humanity, which is just as important as medication. What she demonstrated was quality care.

My Sister Paola

In 1996, my dear sister Paola passed away. It seemed incredible that one of us would die before our parents, but that is the reality of it. She had been sick for a few years with lymphoma, and we had hoped and prayed she would go into remission.

When I saw her in her casket and watched it being carried to her final resting place, the grief I tried to keep inside would not stay there. I tried to be strong when she had talked to me on the phone for the last time, but so much despair was in her young voice. At her funeral, I could not hold my tears any longer. The pain I felt was deep and excruciating. A part of my life had passed away. I would not see her anymore.

Her husband's pain, her children's dry, rigid grief, and my mother's anguish touched me deeply. Dealing with her death when she was still so young was more difficult than I had expected. Yet, witnessing the devastating effect of such a cruel disease has made me better prepared to help others cope when illness afflicts them, both for the patients and their loved ones.

Lonely

One night, I was doing my rounds in the palliative care unit at St. Joseph's. It was a busy night for the unit with the doctor checking on several patients and the nurses giving medication and checking the pumps that administered medications.

I entered one room that had two beds. One patient was asleep, but the other one was in the washroom. By the sounds coming from that small room, I knew the patient was quite agitated. She eventually came out, and I helped her settle back in bed.

"Oh, Barbara, you can't sleep. What can I do for you?" I took her hands in mine.

"I'm thinking of so many things, of my family who should be here. Please, can you stay with me for a while?"

I sat by her bed, quietly stroking her hands and looking at her. She closed her eyes, but I knew she wasn't sleeping. After a while in silence, she said softly, "You know, Mirella, I love you."

I thought of how powerful those words were, but the members of her family should have heard them, not me. Where were they in this woman's hour of need? In the days prior, when Barbara's condition had begun to deteriorate, a social worker and other staff members had called someone from her family. Barbara had a daughter from out of town who said she would come, but we hadn't seen her yet.

This woman was dying, and she was all alone. However, I refused to pass judgment on the reasons for her family's absence, choosing instead to be the one who would fill this woman's need by spending time with her.

I believe in the ministry of presence, and that's what I did late that night with Barbara. I offered my caring presence. I realized how desperate I would feel in her position if my family could not be with me. I sat with her for a time, and her breathing soon became more relaxed. I knew she had fallen asleep, so I left her with a blessing. She died that night. Her last words to me, perhaps to anyone, were words of love.

I do not know if her daughter or anyone else from her family ever came to see her. It was too late now to be concerned about that. I wondered how they would feel knowing that they weren't with her during the last moments of her life. Would they regret it, and would they carry that regret with them until the end of their lives?

Depending on our circumstances, being alone can either be desired or dreaded. We may sometimes be comfortable in our own corner of the world and cherish being only with ourselves, but, other times, isolation can make us sad, self-pitying, and unable to see any blessings around us.

In times of sickness, loneliness hits people the hardest. Having someone nearby who will listen to complaints, the story of the illness, and the hope for better health is a sign to the sufferer that the Lord cares for him or her, as manifested through the care and compassion of another human being. To spend a bad night and know that someone will be there in the morning to hear about it and offer consolation makes one expectant for daylight and spurs the vital feeling of hope.

Thinking of the patient I sat with, I pondered how she might feel if she knew that no one would be there with her as she took her last breath. Might she wish for the presence of a loved one telling her she is loved and will be remembered? To be alone at such a time must be the most painful experience at the end of life. As caregivers, we have an obligation to ensure that those in our care avoid ever having to endure such a possibility. Supporting family and being with patients in their last hours is the mission of palliative care workers.

Mistakes

At times, I have made mistakes or perhaps haven't demonstrated as much compassion toward people as I was capable of. I regret this deeply. It is important for me to examine my actions and evaluate the extent of my mistake. What could I have done differently? How could I repair it?

It may take me a whole sleepless night to get back on track. Certainly, I'm not going to repeat whatever was done improperly. I'm human, too, and, as a human being, I know that no one is perfect, but I strive to overcome those mistakes as best I can.

For many weeks, a close-knit family had maintained a vigil around their mother. Friends and relatives expected and encouraged her to get better, but she did not. Instead, she slowly deteriorated.

One morning, the whole family was called in because the staff saw that her end was imminent. I was with them at the foot of the bed, watching for any sign of distress and approaching death. Some of the family members left the room. Her son and his friends went out to the main hall while her daughter, sister-in-law, and a few other relatives kept their vigil by the bed. Anxiously, they kept asking me if they could do anything, if they should call the nurse or the doctor … something.

Repeatedly, I tried to reassure them that their mother looked comfortable at the moment, and it was only a matter of time for her. Then I saw it happening. Her breathing slowed and became fainter. Her face took on a greenish pallor. It was the moment of death. I approached the side of the bed and rang the bell.

Her daughter screamed at me, "Is this it? Is she dead?" I told her to go call the nurse, and she ran out of the room.

After a few moments, the nurse came in with the rest of the family, who was already weeping. I quickly let the son and daughter come closer to their mother while the nurse told them, "She's still breathing. Say your good-bye to her now."

At those words, I realized I had made a mistake. I had sent the daughter out of the room on her mother's last breath when I should have gone myself to look for her brother and the others and let her stay by her mother's side to say good-bye in those final moments.

I felt guilty and uncomfortable, and I do not know if they realized through their confusion and pain that I hadn't followed procedure. It was not the moment to speak about it, but I later went to the nurses' station and apologized for my thoughtlessness in those precious last moments. The nurses did not think I had done anything wrong, but, rather, I had been quite prompt in summoning the nurse and the rest of the family. To this day, it has not felt right to me, so I have been very careful in subsequent cases to make sure that the family members were present for their loved one's last breath.

In later days, I had the opportunity to apologize to the daughter, but she had not felt anything amiss. Rather, my faithful presence amidst her family touched her.

What Will Happen When I Die?

It is a rare individual who has not asked this question of himself or herself. Rarer still is finding an answer that satisfies. Ultimately, this question will only be answered definitively when death comes. Many people like to talk about it (because it fascinates them), especially when sickness or crisis visits them. Then their mortality becomes so precious and vulnerable.

A man in his fifties asked to see me. He was on the cardiac floor of BGH and recovering from a mild heart attack and a fall down some stairs at home. Because of this accident, he wore a high collar around his neck to help his collarbone and his neck to heal.

He knew quite a lot about the world, life, and the hospital, so we had an interesting conversation. Then he surprised me by asking suddenly, "What happens to me if I die?"

"Well," I answered slowly, "all your functions stop. That much we know. However, nobody has ever come back to tell us what happens to our spirit though. I can only tell you what I know and what I believe."

"But that's what I'm concerned about. I'm concerned what about if everything stops like you said. They put me in the grave under the earth, and then I wake up. What will I do?"

It sounded a bit naïve to me, but I tried my best to answer. "You know, Ron that's why morticians wait several days before they put people in the casket. You can wake up if you want and can." We giggled together. "However, seriously, with modern methods, that does not happen anymore. It may have happened in the past, and you may have seen it happen in movies, but I do not believe it happens anymore, what with all the care and attention they give to the deceased."

"Well, you answered that. Now, I am dead, I am in my coffin, everybody is making a fuss over me gone, and so on. Where am I at this time?"

"Ron, I can only tell you what I know and what I believe. A part of us, our soul, does not die. Our soul makes us what we are. That part goes to the Lord in heaven. Where heaven is, I do not know. We see movies and read in books that heaven is in the sky and hell is below the earth with lots of rocks and flames. I do not know if these places exist anywhere. For me, to be in heaven is to be in the presence of the Lord, to see him, to hear his voice, and to come to know fully all the things I do not know now and would like to know. Hell is darkness, as it is said in the gospels, where there is crying and gnashing of teeth. It is being far from the presence of the Lord forever. That is hell."

"Do you think we will still have pain?"

"I believe life will be so much better and happier when we go to the Lord. The prophets speak of not having any more tears and the days of our sorrow will end. There is a passage in Rev 7:9 (NIV). Let me read it to you."

"After this I looked and there before me was a great multitude that no one could count, from every nation, tribe, people and language, standing before the throne and in front of the Lamb. They were wearing white robes and were holding palm branches in their hands. And they cried out in a loud voice: 'Salvation belongs to our God, who sits on the throne, and to the Lamb.'"

"These are people who have come out of the great tribulation here on earth and have washed their robes, so now they are clean and white in the blood of the Lamb, and they are saved. Pretty powerful, isn't? I believe you and I will join them, if we believe in the salvation of the Lord Jesus Christ."

"Well, chaplain, I have to think of all you have told me. It makes many things clearer and less fearful to me. I guess that, if another attack comes, I will have to be ready to wear my white robe and sing. The singing part I worry about." He chuckled.

He recovered well enough for me to meet him several months later when I was a volunteer in the hospital.

I often talk to people facing death, and I tell them that I believe they will go to a better place than here on earth.

"What if it isn't true?" someone asked.

For me, it is true because Jesus often talked of a better place with him. And I believe firmly in Jesus' words. Perhaps it is childish to imagine heaven as a beautiful garden full of every imaginable flower, cascading fountains, and lovely scents. Perhaps there is the possibility for me to play the organ and sing well, without always coughing, in the presence of the Lord.

He saves me. I am forgiven all wrong things I have said and done in my life because I asked him and he has promised he would. I believe in his promise of eternal life with him in a place where there is joy and beauty.

Chapter 5

That I May Dwell in the House of the Lord Forever

Music from the Chapel

I've had the privilege of working in numerous health-care facilities, and it was a rare case when I found a facility that didn't house a chapel or any such place of worship for the patients, staff, and visitors. It reassured me to know that, no matter how frenetic daily life in the hospital could sometimes get, there was always a place to rest and contemplate the Lord in prayer.

In most cases, the chapel is open to all people, regardless of their faith or race. In some places, it is referred to as the "worship center," thus reinforcing the idea that it is a place where anyone who wants to be there is welcome.

Despite its small size, the chapel at BGH was well used. Staff members would often come there during their break to rest. Visitors waiting to see a doctor or a patient would come and worship with us.

One afternoon, a group of Muslim ladies asked if I knew which way pointed east. One of them had a compass in her purse, and, after much consultation and giggling, we found the direction they wanted, and they turned to pray toward the East. I was very honored that they wanted to come to the chapel to pray for their loved one's health.

At St. Joseph's, we had a very spacious, lovely chapel with a beautiful organ where we conducted weekly worship services. One woman, confined to her wheelchair, expressed to me her joy of being able to come and worship there.

"While I was at home, I hadn't been able to go to our church for a long time. I didn't have anybody who could take me. I was surprised and overjoyed to find a chapel here with a service. It means so much to me to be able to sing and pray with others in a real chapel. Thank you all for making it possible."

Many other residents expressed their joy at being able to worship in a real chapel, even though they were far from their own place of worship and wheelchair-bound. While we were on the second floor, we could often hear music rising through the back stairway from the chapel, and we sometimes heard it when there was no service. Many dedicated pianists, organists, and singers offered the gift of their music that enveloped us during our moments of meditation.

During my years working at this hospital, I began taking organ lessons at home from a patient and accomplished teacher. I spent many moments of pure bliss playing hymns and other simple pieces on that instrument.

On days that I worked at the hospital, I arrived early in the morning, well before my usual start time, and played the organ. Some of the staff told me they listened to me playing. They said how much they enjoyed the music while attending to their work. It made me proud that I could contribute, little by little and with much patient practice on my part, to also offer the ministry of music.

The pianists and organists could see for themselves just how much the patients enjoyed it. Many who came early for the service loved to sit quietly in the chapel and listen to the music.

When I hear music coming from the chapel, I think the Lord is in his temple, waiting for us to come to him with praises and songs and leave behind the concerns of hospital life.

A Place for Everyone

At St. Joseph's, we decided to offer worship services on Sunday mornings, but, because it was not easy to transport patients to the chapel, we used the dining room on the fourth floor. I would set it up for the service, and patients would either wheel themselves in or the staff would bring them in from the third floor. It was very pleasant to gather in the bright room for worship.

For several years, I had pastoral students from McMaster Divinity College working with me as a part of their field program. A requirement of their masters' program was participating with the patients and helping with worship services. I usually invited my pastoral students to lead the service. This was a wonderful opportunity for them to preach and meet and talk with patients in a hospital environment.

An Indian man and his wife were sitting by the fish tank in the hall and watching us prepare for the usual service. I had already met them and knew by our conversation that they were Hindus. The man's wife was very sick. She reclined awkwardly in her geriatric chair. Her face was pale, and illness marked her whole being. Her husband was most concerned about her every movement and moan. He approached me, smiled, and asked if they could attend the service.

"Our services are for everyone. We talk and pray to God and Jesus who loves everyone. You and your wife are most welcome to come and seek them," I answered.

They came and paid careful attention to everything. I gave them a Bible and a songbook and showed them where to look for the passages and songs we would use during the service. Afterward, the husband said with tears in his eyes, "My wife is so very sick, and I have been praying to God to help her. I think God heard me because I have peace now. We will come again to the Christian service."

A Catholic woman expressed her wish to attend. Arrangements were made for her to come even though she was bed-ridden and unable to use a wheelchair. A nurse prepared her for the short trip down the hall, and the nurse and the woman's nephew pushed her bed to the makeshift chapel on the fourth floor. She truly enjoyed that time of worship after spending long hours in her room. She appreciated the music and the prayers most of all.

For several years, we continued the Sunday service with the help of many people like my students, volunteers, pianists, and other staff. They were moments of real intimacy with our Lord when we gathered there to invite him into our lives.

A Sacred Place to Wait

The small chapel at BGH also offered a secluded haven for someone in need of quiet or a restoring of the soul. For several weeks, we had a patient who had a severe stroke that left him with a paralyzed arm. He was unable to walk, speak, or focus on tasks or people. Ron was still in his early forty. When nurses or orderlies helped him into a wheelchair, he tried to move about on his own. He'd try to get it moving with his unaffected arm and foot. Many times, I met him in the corridor. He stared into space with his face downcast and dark, unable to focus.

However, miracles do happen, and, little by little, with the constant care of competent therapists and his own will to improve, he was able to focus on the people around him. Every time I said, "Good morning, Ron, how are you?" he would look at me intently.

His recovery was stunning. We realized he was a very intelligent man by the methods he devised to get his message across. He showed us the exercises he did and how he used his good limbs to strengthen the other ones. He communicated with us by making words and letters with his fingers. One day, he showed me an exercise he did with his good hand on the fingers of the other one. When he finished, he looked at me and smiled proudly with an expression that seemed to say, "What do you think about that?"

I praised and congratulated him. Truly, I was so proud of his improvement. He took my hand and kissed it.

Ron had a respectful and loving relationship with his wife, Helen. She came almost every day. They sat together, holding hands, giving each other a kiss, or just sitting by the window. As she worked on her knitting, she talked with about the plans she was making to adapt their house to his disabilities. It was so good to see them together, happy to be with each other and hopeful for the future.

Ron was soon zipping around the ward, having learned how to quickly turn the wheel of his chair with his good hand. He was so good at maneuvering his wheelchair that he would show other patients how to make better use of theirs.

I often found him at the chapel entrance, being very quiet and waiting for Helen. Through sign language, he would tell me that he could not stay for the service because she was coming just then, but he wanted to listen to me playing the organ. By the time he went home, he was starting to enunciate some easy words and sounds. We knew his earnest desire for recovery and he would continue all his exercises and therapies at home. He had hope for the future.

However, not all patients reacted to their illnesses with the same optimism and hope that Ron did. When I talked to one particularly unhappy patient she always cried. She wanted to be left alone, and she did not mix with the other patients, even at meals, although she could function better than others could and could have even helped some of them.

She always told me how unhappy she was there and did not understand why she could not go home. She could do almost everything by herself, but she had to be supervised while she took a certain medication. She was very unsteady on her feet and in her movements. One morning before chapel, I saw her looking very dejected. Cheerfully, I invited her to the service in the chapel, which was around the corner from her room. No, she was not coming. Too much for her!

Imagine my surprise, when in the middle of the service, she appeared in her wheelchair, smiling a bit. I helped her to get settled with the others and sat at her side during the service. When all was finished, she stayed at her place and listened to the organ. I asked her how she liked it.

She said, "I love it. What a good thing you have here for us, and I did not want it. The music is so beautiful. Thank you for inviting me."

Things changed for her and those around her, too. She began to talk to her roommate and her table companions. She even participated in our hymn singing and enjoyed herself. What a different person she became.

One day, she took my hand and kissed it. "You do so much good for us. God must have a place for you in heaven. I want one, too, so please take me to the chapel every time there is a service. I like to wait there for my place in heaven."

The small chapel continued to bless everyone who came, whether it was staff, patients, or visitors, until the day it was closed and used as a conference room for patients and family. A beautiful new chapel would soon take its place, ready for a new service of witness to the Lord.

Worship Traditions

One of the services that we organized with great care was the distribution of communion, especially at Christmas and Easter. Communion always coincided with one of the hospital's busiest times of the year. Still, we felt it was of great importance to distribute it to those patients who had to stay in the hospital for an extended period of time. To them, partaking of communion meant many things: memories of services in their church, nostalgia, renewal of faith and commitment, or reconciliation with their own church traditions.

Volunteers, clergy, chaplains, and medical staff made the effort to reach every patient who wished to receive communion and gave this task their reverence, respect, and prayer. Clergy from different congregations in town—sometimes up to eight denominations represented—gathered in the chapel for a short time of devotion and prayer, and then they went out to the patients who waited for them.

It was always with an attitude of a good deed completed that the clergy and pastoral volunteers returned, telling me about administering Holy Communion to receptive patients. They had all experienced a new blessing in giving the patients communion and in reflecting on this meaningful act. Once again, we give, but we also receive graciously from our Lord.

I remember another instance of receiving a few days before Christmas when a patient lay awake in the hushed early morning, listening to the holiday music playing softly on the radio at the nurses' station. Such was the case for music on every floor at St. Joseph's, where decorations also contributed to the season.

A figure appeared at the woman's bedside. The woman realized it was Sister Margaret, one of the nuns who worked there. She whispered, "Do you want to receive the sacrament?"

Gladly, the patient received it, and Sister Margaret prayed quietly by her bedside, blessed her, and left in the same respectful manner.

Later that day, I met that woman walking along the corridor. She told me she was getting ready to go home. "You know, chaplain, even though I expect there will be a great feast at home because we are a large family, I had my Christmas celebration quietly this morning when Sister Margaret gave me the Eucharist, the body of Christ. There was silence and reverence around me— only the sound of Christmas music—and I took Christ within me. That was my Christmas moment, no matter how we celebrate it at home all together."

A gentleman sitting by the window in his wheelchair watched the snowflakes dance. The snow fell to the ground softly, covering everything and giving a clean, new appearance to the scenery. I took his hand and sat beside him. I knew he could not go home for Christmas due to his deteriorating condition. There were tears in his eyes while he said, "My minister has been here and gave me communion. I had not received it for a long time, and it comforted me. It made me realize I still have ties with my church. The best thing of all is that the minister sat by me and listened to my life story with great compassion. He wasn't busy or in a rush to go some other place. He had time for me. I cried, and I wasn't ashamed of my tears, even though I'm a man, like I'm not ashamed of them now in front of you, chaplain. They are good for me. It's as if something inside me is free and I'm lighter. The minister prayed with me and blessed me. I'm here waiting for what will happen, and I'm more comfortable inside myself."

And then together we went to God in prayer, thanking him for his blessing on this patient through his minister's visit.

The Bell Ringers' Tradition

It all started when I paid a visit to the mental health unit in BGH one year around Christmastime. The place looked cheerless. Boredom and depression seemed to hang in the air. The therapists tried their best to bring the excitement of sports, activities, games, and conversation to the patients, to create an atmosphere of normalcy among many dysfunctional cases. I thought some music might help to bring cheer in the unit. I asked for guidance from my supervisor and the staff, and then I started to organize a concert.

My church had a group of talented women who played the bells. I had heard the joyful music a few times, and it always filled me with excitement and anticipation of the Christmas event. After several consultations, I arranged for the group to come and give a concert at the hospital.

As the accomplished players went through their repertoire of familiar and joyful tunes, I watched some of the people present. Those who were really not interested showed it through their body language, with their withdrawal and resentment. Evidently, they had come because the staff had told them to or had encouraged them to come, but the joy and meaning in the music touched the majority of patients, visitors, and staff. They clapped and sang softly to themselves, and they smiled and cheered. Joy was with them.

Our efforts were rewarded, and the bell ringer's concert was declared a success, for it boosted the spirits of the patients and staff at a time when joy is very difficult to experience. Burdens do not disappear just because it is Christmas, but hard times can be made more bearable with a few instances of joy.

The bell ringers' concert became a yearly tradition. The event was first moved to the big auditorium where more patients and staff from other units could attend. Then it later changed to the large chapel, a central location for everyone who was a patient or employee there. The ritual brings a lot of joy and hope.

Something else that has also become a tradition is the memorial service. Every other month, we remember patients who have died during that time. It wasn't easy to hold it in the small chapel because it was always so well attended that we would run out of space. These days, in the new and bigger chapel, it is much more comfortable for everyone to listen to good music in that brightly lit room as they remember their loved ones. At times, funeral services were also conducted in the chapel because it was especially meaningful for the family to return to the hospital where their loved one had died and to celebrate that precious life here with the chaplains and the clergy.

Come and Be Still

Along the top of one wall of the chapel at BGH, these words stand out on a banner, "Come and be still." When I enter the chapel, the aura of reverence, peace, and simplicity still surprises me. It is a beautiful chapel built by people who understood its necessity in a hospital, as a place built mainly for the patients and the staff to worship and pray.

The sun pours through its many windows, and light blinds may temper its fierceness on some particularly bright days. The colors on the wall are delicate and blend together harmoniously. Flowers, plants, and banners provide color and freshness, a marked contrast to the rest of the building. This is a place where I love to encounter my Lord and stay with him for a while "to gaze upon the beauty of the Lord."

When I first arrived at the hospital in 1998, I found a small and inviting chapel along with two offices for pastoral care. It was not meant for large services or a large gathering. However, I had a vision. I saw patients in their wheelchairs join with staff and family members in weekly worship services in a larger room.

My supervisor was a very wise lady with great understanding of the need for pastoral care. Together, we talked about my vision. Together, we began to dream. When the administrative staff of the hospital started planning to rebuild parts of the hospital, the architect consulted us, and we shared our dream. A committee was assigned to revamp the pastoral care area, so plans were drawn up, discussed by the committee, and finally approved. My supervisor found the right location for the new quarters, a large, bright, airy space that would give us room for a large chapel, suitable space for offices, and a quiet room. Even a kitchenette was a possibility.

So I began to wait and pray. Years passed, during which many departments in the hospital were transformed as they were renovated. Other spaces became available through the building process. Eventually, the number of patients increased to fill that new space. The hospital was becoming very efficient with state-of-the-art equipment. Meanwhile, I kept reminding the administration of our plans for the chapel. Yes, they were aware of them and would follow them when it was time.

Finally, the time came, and the excitement in me grew when I saw the new chapel being built. Waiting took a lot of patience, but the construction crew knew what we wanted, and they worked speedily.

In past years, we had adapted the small existing chapel to our needs. We used to remove all the chairs to make space for ten to twelve wheelchairs, and we held our weekly services in the small building. The patients and visitors accepted the circumstances graciously, and I must say everyone tried to be helpful, from the cleaning staff to the floor manager. I felt the Lord blessed us all, even if the facilities were limited.

When we had to leave our small chapel for construction, we moved our weekly services to the dining room. The manager and staff generously let us use the room for the worship service, agreeing that the patients still needed it and it would be unfair to them to discontinue services. So many people helped us during the transition as we tried to make the patients' best interests our priority.

My new supervisor, Andrew, dedicated many hours to helping us choose equipment, ensuring that everyone stayed on schedule and helping us prepare for the move. He held the same understanding and need for support as my previous supervisor had shown, and he worked with all of us to fulfill our vision.

The day came when we officially opened the new chapel. Everything was ready. Many hands had worked on countless details. Truly, it was a work of love and respect the laborers felt for the place of worship. Now, it was ready for the people in the hospital to come and spend time apart to meditate in reverence and calm, to find the presence of God away from the bustle and busyness of the hospital. People may find God's presence everywhere, but they often come to the chapel for a special reason.

The Psalmist says, "One thing I ask of the Lord, this is what I seek, that I may dwell in the House of the Lord all the days of my life to gaze upon the beauty of the Lord and to seek Him in His temple" (Ps 27:4 NIV).

God is in our heart. Through the years, my experience has been that people with different burdens, living in diverse situations, will come to the chapel to seek God.

I have seen a mother whose son is on drugs. He is keeping bad company and going down a dangerous road. She seeks God's wisdom and guidance.

A man seeks forgiveness because he has alienated himself from his family through his lifestyle.

An elderly woman sits in a wheelchair because her body is unable to function and take her places she wants to go. She seeks patience.

There is the doctor facing a difficult diagnosis for his patient. He comes to God for inspiration.

There is the nurse who faces ethical decisions in her care of a patient, so she seeks courage. The Psalmist says we come to God's temple, such as the chapel at BGH, "to gaze upon the beauty of the Lord." I pause and gaze not only at the loveliness of the building, but also at how it enhances the intimacy of God's relationship with me and each one of his children. There is a divine beauty in it. In the prayers we whisper in this chapel, we find the glory of God all around us.

Today the chapel—also called the worship center—is open to everyone who seeks refuge from the world. It embraces every person from every land, every condition of life, every religion, and every culture. There are people from every walk of life whose own understanding of a supreme being is accepted. The chapel has been decorated in such a way that no distinctive religious symbols of any one faith predominate. It is there for the entire world to come and visit.

Chaplains Bob and Wes currently head up the pastoral care team. They remind me of lighthouse guardians who keep watch. They prepare the services and make the chapel available for many staff and community events as well. They keep the light burning in the hospital, inviting all who see it to come and warm their souls. Both men are very talented and dedicated to their tasks. I have realized how the Lord blesses their efforts to keep pastoral care on the forefront of hospital life. Faithfully, they invite and help people daily to come to the chapel and seek the Lord.

As I conclude this writing about my reflections as a hospital chaplain, I feel I have been blessed by the opportunity to touch many people and remind them that the Lord is not only in his temple, but also very real in their lives.

Chapter 6

Place Me like a Seal on Your Heart

The Shimmering Stream

It is a crystal clear summer day, and everything is still. I gaze upon my surroundings from the deck behind my home and smell the gentle fragrance of lavender wafting up from below. I also detect the scent of a beautiful lilac-colored rose that blooms several times each growing season. Far in the distance, among the trees, the vibrant flicker of many points of light coming from a nearby creek that shimmers in the sunlight dazzles me. It isn't always visible. There are times when all is dark among the trees. Then suddenly, as a diamond catches the light, the glinting radiance appears again. It makes everything look precious and creates a tranquil, peaceful environment, perfect for meditation and reflection.

The fruition of this book is possible, in large part, because of many people who have been influential in my life since I was very young and whom I have placed like a seal over my heart for so many years. They have enriched my life by their example, their faith in me, and, above all, their care and love.

Like the shimmering water among the trees near my property, so, too, have they appeared as lights in my life. There have been moments where the darkness has been strong and where people would seem to disappear, but then they appear, sparkling like jewels. My life is so much richer for having known them and listened to them.

There have been many of these such jewels. Because I have kept these people precious in my heart, I would like to introduce them to you, dear reader. It is fitting that I begin with my father as he, too, was a minister. He has influenced me since I was very little, as far back as the Second World War.

I Remember My Father

Memories of my father flood my soul these days. Some are positive, and some are negative, but they may give you a picture of the person my father was. I have been thinking of him a lot, trying to assess my feelings for him and attempting to understand him. I must admit that there were times I loved him only because that was what I had been taught. It wasn't a feeling that sprang from deep within my heart.

One of the earliest memories I have of him is being carried on his shoulders as he climbed the mountains near our home in Torino, Italy. I must have been about three years old at the time. World War II had started the year before I was born, and we were eventually forced to leave Torino from time to time for the safety of the mountains because the Allies had started a bombing campaign in Italy. My uncle was the minister of a small church in a little mountain village, and we lived with him and his family in the parsonage. One Sunday, we were at a worship service in Torino when an alarm sounded, warning us that the bombardments had started. My father was thirty-three, young and strong. He carried me on his shoulders and ran toward the mountains. We sang an old hymn, "Beulah Land," as we ran to safety. I felt secure and protected by my strong dad.

While he was working for Fiat, he started theological studies with my grandfather, so he was able to help my uncle in his church, commuting from Torino every day despite the bombardments.

By the side of my uncle's church, there was a big bush of fragrant red roses, which I smelled every time I entered the church. I once saw my father bring a rose from that very bush to my mother. At the time, I didn't understand the full meaning of that act, but I sensed something very good and touching in it.

At the end of the war, we returned to Torino. My father finished his studies for the ministry. He was ordained and then sent to a church situated in the "heel" region of Italy. Those were hard times of change for all of us, but he built that church into a strong witness for that city. It was then that conflicts between my father and I started and lasted until I grew up.

I remember watching him as he stood at the pulpit, preaching on Isa 35:8 (NIV), "And a highway will be there; it will be called the Way of Holiness." Though I was young, that sermon had a great impact on me, as did the firmness of his convictions and his faith. I vowed to walk along the holy way all of my life, to be with the people I loved, and to meet the Lord face to face. And I have always been thankful to my father for guiding me in that direction and giving me the example to follow.

As I grew older though, there were many disagreements between us that grew very violent at times. I saw and felt things in a certain way. When they were at odds with those of my father, I expressed myself angrily. In turn, it made him very angry, too. We would argue, and he would punish me to try to tame the rebelliousness he saw in me. I remember how desperate I felt that he did not understand me. He did not like me in the way he liked my sister, and he did not love me as much as he loved my other siblings. When I tried to explain to him my struggle to be better, he would point out that my soul was black, I had a heart of stone, and I was uncaring and insensitive to the others. Otherwise, I would not cause so much pain, especially to my mother. I felt so utterly desperate and unworthy of living with no one to help me.

When I was seventeen, I fell in love with a young man in my church. Even though this person was preparing for the ministry, my father never allowed me to date him because he thought I was too young, too romantic, and unable to see that the man was unsuitable for me. I did not date until I went to the seminary. Even there, I was very hesitant to accept dates because, in the back of my mind, there was always the thought that my father would not approve.

Two years later, I left home for England. I was nineteen and on my own for the first time. I felt that my father finally trusted me enough to let me go so far from home alone. That meant cutting my ties with my home and him. I returned home only for short periods of time until I left for Canada when I was even more on my own. It felt good to be by myself and enjoy the freedom to be my own person in a community of other young people.

I never felt he that entirely approved of me even though I did well at the seminary in Switzerland. Every time something positive was said about me, he always pointed out my rebellious attitude toward him. But he was proud of the fact that I had learned English fairly well. I was his interpreter when he preached in the chapel of the nearby American air base.

If he did praise me, it was always qualified with the advice that I do something about my temper and my faith. He never thought I had a strong faith. However, he believed I was determined to achieve whatever I had set out to do. When I started university again, he encouraged me all the time because he believed in the goodness of education, being a self-made scholar himself. He supported me in my ministry financially and with his encouragement.

He mellowed somewhat toward the end of his life, but even his failing health did not abate his fiery spirit much. He felt he had been hard on his children, especially toward my brother and me. He felt he had tried too hard to mold us into his image.

Sometimes, when I think of the way he treated me, I feel angry and hurt. I had a very difficult childhood and a very unhappy adolescence. He took a lot of freedom from me and the right to express myself and be my own person. However, I have to admit that I was a difficult daughter to deal with and required a lot of patience and understanding. What I have come to appreciate about my father is how courageous he was for standing by his convictions at any cost, even when they caused conflict with others.

What I have always admired about him is his strong faith in God that supported him. I still picture him in the morning at his desk with his head reverently bent in prayer. I am thankful that he set me on the "holy way" at an early age. My love, respect, and sense of obedience for him have kept me vigilant from not deviating from that path too often. I wanted to walk along it with all those I love.

The last time I saw him, he was standing with my mother on the threshold of their home in North Carolina. As I got in the car, I told him, "I will see you next summer. Keep well."

I saw him pointing upward to heaven. That is the way I remember him, pointing to where he is now with my mother and my sister. I regret I didn't have more time to have a good talk with him, explaining many things and showing him my love and respect. But I believe he knows it now.

When he died in, I went back to North Carolina to lay him to rest. Seeing him in his coffin gave me a sense of finality. A part of my life was finished. Looking down at him, I became aware of how peaceful and at rest he looked. This verse from Matt 25:21 (NIV) came to mind, "Well done, good and faithful servant: … Come and share your master's happiness." I'm convinced he has come to the end of the holy way and did indeed meet his master.

The Man from Halifax

A deep cloud of weariness and hopelessness hung over my life one winter. It was extremely cold, and I had much to do as a home missionary in Montreal. I was teaching English as a Second Language to immigrants, and the number of students, especially those of Italian descent, increased weekly.

I was very tired of my life without respite, fun, and diversion. The years were passing me by, and I could not see any instance of the romance I dreamed of in my life. The thought of remaining single all my life did not appeal to me. It saddened me deeply to see some of my friends getting engaged and then married. I was tired of being on my own.

I needed help to teach the increasing number of students in the teaching centers I had opened, so I sent a bulletin to the Baptist churches in Montreal to ask for teachers.

There was a good response for some of the centers. Another message indicated there was "a man from Halifax" who had just arrived in town and was willing to come to my teaching facility in the west end. The man phoned me. He seemed quite pleasant, so we agreed to meet at the café of one of my friends. I thought he sounded well educated and well spoken. I thought he was probably married and already had a family.

Curious about this man, I went to the café on a very cold afternoon. I was very glad and excited to have some help. As I entered the café, I saw it was almost empty, except for a young man sitting at a table and two other gentlemen in a corner who were reading the paper.

With hesitation, I stood at the door. The young man got up and came toward me. "Are you the missionary, Miss Coacci?"

I nodded, shook his hand, and introduced myself. I was pleasantly surprised and a bit shy. He invited me to his table. Over coffee, he explained how he had just arrived from Halifax that week to take a new job in Montreal. Being single and new to the city, he had gone to Westmount Baptist Church. When he read my appeal for teachers in the bulletin, he thought he could help me. Years later, he told me that, because I was a missionary, he had thought of me as an elderly lady and had been pleasantly surprised to meet a pretty, young lady.

Being an immigrant himself, he understood how our students felt when they arrived in Canada. He had come from Holland, and he spoke excellent English. He proved to be a good teacher to our students. They liked him very much and responded to him. So did I. I found him increasingly attractive and pleasant. After a few months, we were dating. God had taken care of me, and my prayers had been answered. My life was now under a clear blue sky, and joy was in my heart.

We have been married for many years, and we are good friends and companions to each other. Ernest has helped immensely with the children, my studies, and work. He was always there, patiently driving me to the train that took me to school, doing errands for me, and assisting me with household chores, except for cooking, a task he has never warmed to. And I prefer it that way.

He's the type of person who always strives to make life easier for those close to him, not only for me, but also for his mother, his friends, and his children. His greatest hobbies are bird-watching and photography. He excels at both of them, and he has enriched my life with his knowledge and appreciation of nature. God had his plan for us when he sent Ernest from Halifax to meet me.

What has also been a great comfort and support for me is Ernest's great faith. He sees God in every inch of nature, and that outlook inspires him to be faithful to his God as he serves in countless volunteer endeavors.

While going to catch the train to Toronto one morning, I complained how I wasn't feeling so great, how I didn't know if I would make it with my studies, and how I felt very weak. The sky was ablaze with the rising sun, a stunning spectacle of power.

"See that sky?" Ernest asked. "It's a way for God to say, 'I am here. I am in control.'"

An Incomparable Mentor

When I was sixteen, the Baptist Union of Italy opened a school in Rome to prepare young girls to serve in the Baptist churches and communities. The Southern Baptist Convention of USA, which had sent several missionaries to Italy to help the Baptist Union after the war, supported the school.

One of those missionaries was Miss Wingo, the director of the Bethany School for Girls. She had come from Louisiana and learned Italian well enough to be able to teach us New Testament history and other classes. The other teachers were Italian, and they all contributed to improving our knowledge of the Bible and Christian life in a church, but Miss Wingo instilled in me a strong love for the Bible by the clear, concise way she explained the stories and concepts. As she presented them, the biblical characters seemed to come alive in our classroom. I prepared myself carefully for the exams at the end of the semester, enjoying the notes I took in class.

She believed in me as an intelligent and wise young lady who needed to be understood and loved. When I told her I believed I was a very bad person, she had tears in her eyes.

She said, "Nobody could be that bad, my dear. I think perhaps your family sometimes made you feel bad without realizing it. Always remember that God loves you as you are, in spite of the fact that you do not see yourself as a good person. Learn to accept God's love for you."

She had great compassion and tenderness. At one time, I suffered for weeks with a terrible toothache, but I didn't complain. I just took some medication and kept going with my duties and studies. She asked me one day how I was feeling, so I told her about my toothache. She promptly phoned the dentist and took me to him. I never forgot her promptness in helping me, and she looked after me like a mother would her daughter. She sometimes reminded me of my mother.

Miss Wingo was also instrumental in providing a scholarship for me to go to the Baptist Seminary at Rüschlikon in Zurich, Switzerland, where I pursued more biblical and theological graduate studies. It was a delight to have someone behind me, who, like my dear mother at home, believed in my potential and saw goodness, intelligence, and wisdom in me. It helped me to nurture these qualities and grow strong with them.

Miss Wingo knew love and must have suffered for it because she understood well when I had a relationship with a young man who lived far away from us. I had a painful time at that age because I had fallen deeply in love with a young man of my church in Pordenone, Italy, but I had a tepid response from him. Miss Wingo encouraged me to keep my correspondence with him and never lose faith in God's will for my life, whatever it may be. Eventually, we had a relationship for a few years.

In the evening, we girls gathered in our pajamas and dressing gowns in her sitting room to talk about the events of the day. Then we would pray together with her. It was a time of deep, spiritual intimacy with each other and our Heavenly Father, and it blessed us for the night.

I'm sure Miss Wingo left a mark in all the girls she taught, as she did for me, for she helped me grow more mature in faith during the two years I spent in that school. I'm sure she's with the Lord now, but

I still feel her impact in so many parts of my life, especially in continuing to believe that there is goodness also in me and God loves everyone, as she taught me to accept.

Mentoring Friends

The Rüschlikon Baptist Seminary in Zurich welcomed students from all over the world and instructed them in theological studies for the ministry. I felt very fortunate to be there and pursue mine. Classes were conducted in English, so one of the first requirements was to become proficient in another language. However, the international representation at the seminary meant that different languages were spoken there, and that sparked great enthusiasm to learn other tongues. Small groups were established where a language other than English was taught.

I became quite interested in learning German, so I joined a small group of three students under a tutor named Wiard. He had a great sense of humor and thought of funny ways to help us with our phrasing. It was a good time for me to learn German because I was planning to spend my summer in Munich at a center for Christian girls where I would work to pay for a trip through Europe. I learned fast, and I was able to follow the Sunday sermons delivered in German in our chapel. I also started to sing German songs. Wiard became an invaluable tutor there, too.

He was a talented organist and willing to share his gift. We spent many hours in the chapel, rehearsing Italian and German songs that I sometimes had the courage to sing during our daily chapel meditation service. My knowledge of German and music was growing fast, thanks to our tutor.

Wiard had graduated summa cum laude at the end of his university training. He married and continued his studies in theology at the University of Zurich and other universities in Germany, eventually earning his doctorate and becoming a professor of theology at Hamburg Seminary. He and his wife had a little girl, Dorothea, whom I babysat between classes.

I loved this young family very much. They were most helpful and supportive of me in my studies and my life at the seminary. Not everything was simple and rosy, and I often went to them for counseling and encouragement. They were always available to help me.

In my last year at the seminary, we intensified my German lessons and my voice lessons. To repay Wiard for his kind help,

I taught him a bit of Italian. Being extremely smart, he picked it up easily and, of course, found funny ways to speak also in Italian. We had a lot of fun, especially when he addressed his poor wife and daughter in Italian, and they did not know what was going on. My love of music, especially organ music, has grown in me through the years. Wiard opened my heart to it and guided me through it with great kindness. I thank him today when I play the organ for that valuable early direction in my life.

I graduated from the seminary with honors and then headed for Montreal with my small wealth of knowledge and great enthusiasm to begin my work as a home missionary in 1965. Being young and inexperienced, I had many dreams but a lot of frustration at not being able to realize them. The New Canadian Committee of the Baptist Churches looked after me and another missionary in Montreal. We were both affiliated with Temple Baptist Church and worked with its minister, Reverend Paul Stevens. There were many days of hard work with the immigrants who had flocked to Canada and needed help with the English language in order to integrate into Canadian life. We started many teaching centers and support groups for them, helping them in every way we could.

Reverend Stevens had an innate understanding of their needs. He guided us and established Temple Baptist Church as a center for helping families and children. At a church-owned farm outside of Montreal, he organized camps for young people, retreats for adults, and Bible studies and prayer groups geared to the comprehension level of Canada's newer citizens. In him, I found great compassion and understanding for people coming from another country. From him, I learned how to deal with their needs rather than my intentions and plans.

One evening, we were coming home from a visit and Bible study at the home of some immigrants. It was snowing. I was tired and cold and remarked how lazy those people were. I had to transport them everywhere in my car and always translate for them. They did not seem to learn to do anything for themselves.

Reverend Stevens was clearing the wipers of the car. He looked at me seriously and said, "Maybe we have to lower our expectations and not anticipate so much from our work. It will be in God's time."

I have kept those humbling words in my heart for all these years. When I start to get impatient in my work and expect things to go my way, right away, I recall what he said. I know I have to lower my expectations and trust in God's timing.

Temple Baptist Church has remained a church for people from many countries, following the guidelines Reverend Stevens set years ago. It's still thriving and spreading its witness to the strangers who come to Montreal. The church becomes a lighthouse for them in their transition to a foreign land.

Following in Their Footsteps

My field education professor at Emmanuel College in Toronto suggested I enter the Clinical Pastoral Education (CPE) program at Sick Children's Hospital, which was close to the college. When I started the training, I was very confused about what it entailed and what to expect in a hospital. I was quite unfamiliar with hospital life and was not sure how I would take it.

We had a congenial group of people for CPE and started working together. My supervisor, Mary, was a United Church minister who was quite open about herself and her life. Weeks of tutoring under her leadership helped me to understand what chaplaincy was all about, what it involved, and what it required of me. I learned from Mary that a good pastoral visit did not always have to involve prayer and that it could be a good visit without talking about God and religion. This stunned some of the students. What were we there for then? But I started to learn a new way of visiting people in need without becoming emotionally involved with them. I learned about spirituality. Later on, in other institutions, people liked the fact that I'm not a bleeder for people. I'm there for them without exaggerating my efforts to "save" them. Mary spoke about spirituality; how we can connect with people's thoughts and feelings, let them talk about what troubles them inside, and examine their emotions in this state in life; and how they view their sickness at this time in their life.

It was a world of discovery for me, entering into people's inner lives and helping them to sort it out. I started to look at Mary as a role model. Perhaps one day I would be like her as a chaplain.

The simple way she used to approach people appealed to me. She taught me that I didn't have to start a big conversation with someone after I introduced myself. I could just carry on a normal conversation, as someone truly interested in how a patient was progressing in the hospital, and then listen actively to the feelings behind their words and watch for signs that something might be troubling the person. Mary's instruction guided me through those months at Sick Kids Hospital until

I came to the point where I realized that being a chaplain was like "coming home" for me. It was what I wanted to do for the rest of my life, to walk alongside the sick people and support them as far as I could. Having started on the road to chaplaincy, I took more CPE courses at other hospitals. The road was not easy as I had a family to look after. I lived so far from the hospitals that offered the courses. A friend of mine, a talented artist, gave me one of her paintings depicting a road flanked by trees and intermittent patches of shadows and light dotting the road. I still have that painting. It reminds me that we each have moments of shadows and light on the roads we travel, but the important thing is to stay on the road.

My children were teenagers by that time. They were in school, and I managed to be available when they needed me. My husband helped me to reach the hospital in time and be home in the afternoon.

I felt God strongly leading me in my new career, so I started the CPE courses at Whitby Psychiatric Hospital, despite my fear of working in a psychiatric hospital, a facility in which I had never been before. My supervisor was very helpful in making things easier for his students that, after a while, I realized I was enjoying myself. Together with the other students and the other chaplains, my supervisor led us to consider the patients as children of God. He loved them, too, and recognized they were just people like us with something gone wrong in their brains and nervous systems.

After a while, it was easy to visit with them, even with those who did not look attractive, because I had learned to see a person, a human being, rather than a mental patient. I learned to sit still and listen attentively to patients' stories. Our supervisor led us in worship with them and trained us how to prepare a devotional for them. I was learning fast, and all aspects of chaplaincy presented to me fascinated me. At the end of the course, my supervisor surprised me by saying that I was his stellar student. I had been able to absorb a lot of knowledge on how to be a chaplain in an institution, working well with patients, staff, and administration. When I left, I felt I had many friends there and people whom I esteemed and respected.

My theological studies and CPE training were ending. The time came to consider my ordination. Reverend Bruce Coombe, the minister of my church in Oshawa, was my supervisor for the year of preparation. He had been instrumental in getting me started in my theological studies at Emmanuel College. He knew who to contact to get things started for me. Because I felt so comfortable and happy at Whitby, my credentials committee suggested I do my year of internship there under Bruce's supervision. I'd had many years of church experience because I had always been involved in many activities at my church. I needed clinical experience though, and I was very happy to return to Whitby. Bruce was very wise and practical. Because of my previous involvement in church activities, he permitted me to lead many Sunday services and to preach occasionally. I also led the service and preached at the Whitby chapel, where I sometimes also sang for the patients.

I soon became less nervous on the pulpit. Bruce remarked, "You know, Mirella, you show a love of worship when you do the service."

Time went fast, and, as my ordination approached, I was quite anxious. What if the church council didn't accept me? What if they asked me difficult questions that I couldn't answer? As I talked these things over with Bruce, he said quietly, "Mirella, why do you not leave everything in the Lord's hands? Just leave it there. Do not take it back."

So I took his advice, and everything proceeded smoothly. I was ordained to work in chaplaincy as I desired. Bruce had steadily led me through that process with gentleness and an unwavering faith in my abilities, and that trust and confidence delighted me, as I now felt ready to start in my ministry.

After my ordination, I began my internship as a chaplain at Toronto Western Hospital. It was a very tough and stressful year, but I ended it feeling I had grown into a strong, determined person. Dreams beckoned on the horizon, but I did not know that, little by little, with patience, steady work, and a lot of faith in the Lord, many of them would come true.

Leading Wisely

During both my training in CPE and also in my career, I have worked with many outstanding supervisors, and I have kept them precious in my memories. Not only did I learn a lot from them, but I worked harmoniously with them, finding them not only congenial colleagues but also friends.

The fall of 1991 was a very trying one for me. I had finished my chaplaincy training, and I was ready to enter the race. However, after continuous setbacks, I was getting very discouraged. Then one day, I received a call from St. Joseph's in Brantford, Ontario. I had waited so long for an opportunity, and, all of a sudden, there it was! My whole life and that of my family changed, but we took it in stride and embraced this fortuitous event. I could finally settle into my career, relax, and enjoy being at St. Joseph's to answer my call.

Through this new profession and position as chaplain, I received recognition of my abilities and offered financial security to my family. My supervisor, Kathy, worked closely with me, gently easing me into the job. In her, I found a trustworthy colleague and friend. She taught me how to note the details in patients' stories because they would lead me to a greater knowledge and understanding of their needs.

Precise in her work, Kathy was very attentive to the patients and their families. She interacted well with the staff. She reached out and offered compassion and knew when someone among us was having a difficult time. She was there to help us through it. She always seemed to go beyond her assigned duties. What attracted me most though was her honesty and integrity. She was a true Christian in all aspects of her work.

Now St. Joseph's had three chaplains: Kathy, Sister Margaret, and me, along with volunteers who regularly assisted with pastoral care. We worked together in harmony and friendship, supporting each other for many years until the hospital was closed and we each went our own way.

When St. Joseph's was closed, I was offered a position as coordinator of pastoral care with the Brant Community Health Care System, also known as Brantford General Hospital or BGH, in Brantford. Kathy came to work with me, too, for a while, and we enjoyed working together again, each in our own positions. Our supervisor proved to be a true ally and friend. She had great respect and understanding for pastoral care, and together we were able to rebuild it and give it a more meaningful role within the hospital's services. Our committee, consisting of several clergy and other staff from the hospital, met over several weeks to reorganize pastoral care and formulate plans for the future, eventually preparing for a new chapel and quarters for the department. Those were very exciting times, and, under the competent and sympathetic leadership of my supervisor, we achieved many goals.

Changes were afoot, and, eventually, Kathy and my supervisor left the hospital. Today, Kathy continues her work as a chaplain in another hospital with the same diligence, honesty, and Christian professionalism. I continued my work alone, but, by this time, it became evident that we would require at least one more chaplain.

The hospital budget would not allow for this, however, but my faith in the Lord gave me the energy and insight to carry on by myself. I was able to organize a network of pastoral volunteers, lay visitors, and clergy. They helped me in my visits, clerical duties, and during worship services. I was grateful to have them come and help every week.

My new supervisor, Andrew, had the same affinity with pastoral care as his predecessors. Together, we reviewed the pastoral care department with the clergy and the volunteers. Because the existing chapel was no longer safe to use, it was closed. Andrew was very helpful during the many moves to various locations in the hospital, due to construction of the new chapel and offices.

When we were looking at our existing budget one day, we realized we had some money left over before the new budget would be prepared. I wished to have banners in the chapel, and Andrew gave permission to buy some. I went to the city of Kitchener and found a big sale there at one of the religious bookstores. I bought two beautiful ones at a bargain price that allowed me to stay within the budget.

I was so excited that I decided to play a joke on Andrew. We'd had tense times trying to stay within budget limits and still buy beautiful accessories and furniture for the chapel. I phoned him, chatting away how good the banners would look and that I had paid $2,000 for them.

"What? Stay there! I want to see them!" he shouted.

He must have sprinted from his office to mine because he arrived there much sooner than I expected. I showed him the banners, going into great detail about how beautifully they were stitched, but I could see he was worried. So I presented him the bill, and he gave a big sigh of relief.

"I could wring your neck," he said.

The banners look wonderful in their place in the chapel, and I chuckle when I think how I worried my poor supervisor.

Through his steady leadership, we came through the construction phase without difficulty, and the day came when Andrew and I planned the opening ceremony for our new quarters and the beautiful chapel.

He said something that delighted me. "This makes me look good."

Even though he, the director of the mental health unit, has a heavy responsibility with many staff reporting to him and the pastoral care portfolio is small, Andrew considers pastoral care to be of great importance in the life of the hospital. He was always ready to help me unravel some problems, to listen to me when I voiced my concerns, and to go to the administrators with my requests. Like my previous supervisors, he proved to be a diligent colleague and a good friend.

The hospital has two new chaplains now and a number of volunteers who work with Andrew. He gives them all of his attention and support, as he did for me. They work together as a team and continue to make the pastoral care department recognized and an asset to the hospital.

Friends at Heart, Buddies

When Sister Margaret retired from St. Joseph's, we needed another chaplain. The sisters sent us one of their youngest nuns. To my surprise and delight, it was Sister Kathleen, whom I had met in previous years and highly respected. Sister Kathleen was a teaching supervisor, and she had finished her training at St. Joseph's. At the time, we had a CPE unit there with different students assisting us each year. They had all enjoyed Sister Kathleen's leadership, becoming well-trained chaplains as a result of it.

Kathleen has a wonderful sense of humor, and I soon gravitated toward her gentle and caring approach. We visited the patients in the palliative care unit, and, as we worked together, we became good friends, often sharing our experiences and advice with each other. Although work in the hospital was challenging at times, we found moments of relief when Kathleen and I met in the cafeteria for coffee or lunch. There we shared a bit of fun with other staff members. We enjoyed lunch time in the cafeteria and shared the laughter, social times with co-workers, and good food for which St. Joseph's was known.

The ups and downs of hospital life were smoothed out with Kathleen's arrival. Little by little, I found out that I had found a soul mate. We thought very much alike on the kind of care the patients needed and on theological matters, even though I was Baptist and Kathleen was Catholic. Because of my openness and help with Catholic patients, both my supervisor Kathy and Kathleen defined me as "a Catholic Baptist." Because of that, there was always a lot of teasing when I assisted in preparing mass, the Eucharist, memorial services, and so on.

When I was a child in south Italy, there was a time when I was the only Protestant child in my school. All the other students were Catholic. I got along well with all of them and the teachers, but, when the priest or the nun arrived for religious education, I was always very apprehensive. What would happen if they questioned me and I could not answer? Just the sight of the black gown made me very anxious. As I grew, however, these feelings disappeared so much that I was not all surprised when I worked at St. Joseph's that one of my best friends was a nun. She was my buddy!

We enjoyed walks around the hospital's neighborhood during our lunch breaks, when we enjoyed the sun, fresh air, flowers, and freedom like two young girls without worries. We talked to each other like sisters about many things in our lives. It was a grand time to be together. At times, we prayed together, which was remarkable because I can remember thinking when I was a child that I would one day be sharing prayer with a nun. Kathleen is like me. We each have a deep spirituality, but do not talk about it all the time, do not fuss over it, and do not overburden other people with it. We derive our communion from it and are able to share our devotional life because of it.

Though the paths of our lives don't cross nearly as much as before, we still keep in touch. We meet for coffee or lunch, we lean on each for support and understanding, and we share our burdens with one another. Most of all, we keep each other in our prayers.

My life is easier and quite pleasant now at home with Ernest. We enjoy our home and the activities we choose and like. But Kathleen is still working hard for her parish, carrying burdens of loneliness and struggles.

"Pray for me," she always says. And I feel such an honor to be her friend and be able to recommend her to the Lord. That's sharing our faith and love for each other.

Always on Call

When I was a child and dreamed of writing a book one day, I envisioned years of labor, stacks of paper, and continuous writing. This book has been a labor of love, which has filled my life with joy. I hope it may bring inspiration and help in some reader's life. I have let the Lord inspire me. And now what is in store for me?

There is my lovely home to enfold me with comfort. Together, my husband and I enjoy a peaceful, serene life. We have worked and followed in the Lord's footsteps all our lives. We have raised a good family, and now we enjoy our rest. I will continue to write, as this activity is a source of enjoyment in my life. We will travel also to other countries, as circumstance allows us. We will keep our family and dear friends close to us because they enrich our life.

Both Ernest and I are concerned and saddened by the situation in our world. We would like to help on a large scale, but we cannot. We spend time in prayer because we know our Lord has the power to change the world and to change people, and we hope this will happen.

With these hopeful thoughts about the future, I place this book in God's hands for him to use as an instrument for the betterment of any who read it.

Although I am retired now, I still welcome every opportunity to offer a sympathetic ear to family, friends, neighbors, and any and all who need to talk to someone about his or her difficulties or joys. I'm quite pleased to be able to speak on occasion at meetings or religious functions or sing during a worship service. I also volunteer at BGH, transporting wheelchair-bound patients to and from the weekly worship service in the chapel.

As I am able to carry on these activities for people, I realize with delight that I still am and always will be "on call for God."

Suggested Additional Readings

Augsburger, D. *Pastoral Counseling across Cultures*. Louisville, Ky.: Westminster John Knox Press, 1986.

Boisen, Anton T. *Out of the Depths*. New York: Harper & Brothers, 1960.

Bowen, M. "Family Reaction to Death." In *Living Beyond Loss: Death in the Family*, edited by F. Walsh and M. McGoldrick. New York: W.W. Norton & Co, 1991.

Burr, W., S. Klein, and associates. *Reexamining Family Stress: New Theory and Research*. Thousand Oaks, Calif.: Sage Publications, Inc., 1994.

Clinebell, H. *Counselling for Spiritually Empowered Wholeness*. Binghampton, N.Y.: Haworth, 1995.

Griffith, M.E. *Spiritual Resources in Family Therapy*. New York: Guilford Press, 1999.

Holland, Jimmie C., MD, and Sheldon Lewis. *The Human Side of Cancer: Living with Hope, Coping with Uncertainty*. Harper Collins Publishers, 2000.

Ilardo, Joseph, and Carol R. Rothman, PhD. *I'll Take Care of You: A Practical Guide for Family Caregivers*. New Harbinger Publications, Inc., 1999.

Moore, T. *Care of the Soul*. New York: Harper Perennial, 1994.

O'Connor, T. "Diversity in the Pastoral Relationship: An Evaluation of the Helping Style Inventory." *The Journal of Pastoral Care* 49(4) (1995): 365–374.

Peel, Donald. *The Ministry of Listening*. Anglican Book Centre, Toronto, Canada, 1980.

Peterson, Sheryl B. *The Indispensable Guide to Pastoral Care*. Cleveland: The Pilgrim Press, 2008.

About the Author

Figure 1. Photo by Ernest van der Zyl.

Mirella was born in the midst of World War II in Torino, Italy, the second daughter of a Baptist minister. Though she grew up in a Baptist environment, she had many friends among the Roman Catholic population, preparing her to be sensitive to different cultures and beliefs as an adult. From an early age, her dream was to be a writer one day, and she has been able to fulfill that dream in her retirement.

After she finished her theological training in Switzerland in 1965, she immigrated to Canada. While living in Montreal, Quebec, she worked for five years as a home missionary under the auspices of the Baptist Women of Ontario and Quebec. She married and raised her family in Montreal, Quebec, and Oshawa, Ontario.

In 1984, she returned to university and chose to study theology at Emmanuel College, Victoria University, in Toronto. She graduated with a master of divinity degree in 1988. The following year, she was ordained to the ministry with the Baptist Convention of Ontario and Quebec. During those years, she found that God's call on her life was to chaplaincy. Consequently, she worked in several hospitals while completing her training as a certified chaplain.

She was eventually called to Brantford, Ontario, where she worked as a chaplain at St. Joseph's Hospital and later at Brantford

General Hospital (BGH) until she retired in 2005. During her career, she spent more than twenty years in chaplaincy duties, enjoying all the opportunities God provided to help people in need of spiritual assistance.

Mirella makes her home in Mt. Pleasant, Ontario, with her husband Ernest, an avid bird-watcher and skilled photographer.